■ THE NEW IMMIGRANTS ■

Mexico

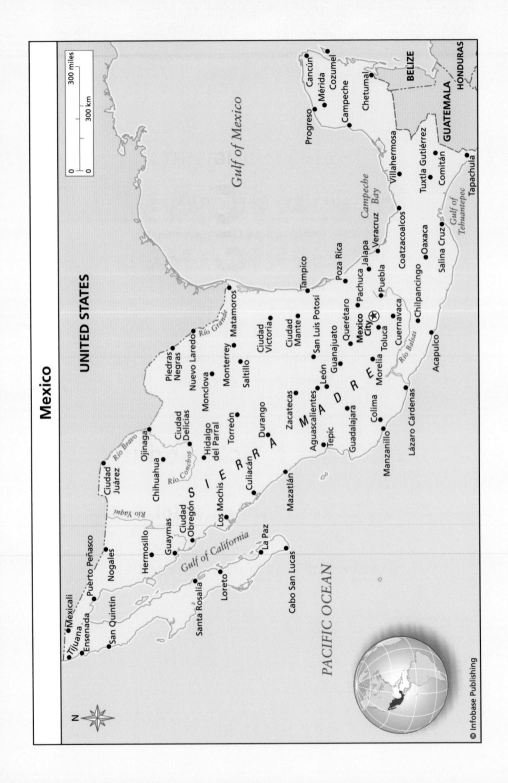

© Infobase Publishing

THE NEW IMMIGRANTS

MEXICAN
AMERICANS

Michael J. Schroeder

Series Editor: Robert D. Johnston

Associate Professor of History,
University of Illinois at Chicago

CHELSEA HOUSE
PUBLISHERS
An imprint of Infobase Publishing

I am very grateful to Nora Faires for her support, encouragement, and smart and helpful comments. I would also like to thank my daughter Sarah Elizabeth Schroeder (age 16), my son Timothy Delehanty Schroeder (age 12), and their friend Michelle Garcia (age 12).

Frontis: Mexico is located just south of the United States and is home to approximately 107 million people. According to the 2000 U.S. census, more than 26 million Americans are of Mexican descent.

Mexican Americans

Chelsea House
An imprint of Infobase Publishing
132 West 31st Street
New York NY 10001

Library of Congress Cataloging-in-Publication Data
Schroeder, Michael J.
  Mexican Americans / Michael J. Schroeder
      p. cm. — (New immigrants)
  Includes bibliographical references and index.
  ISBN 0-7910-8785-9 (hardcover)
1. Mexican Americans—History. 2. Mexican Americans—Social conditions.
3. Immigrants—United States—History. 4. Immigrants—United States—
Social conditions. 5. United States—Emigration and immigration—History. 6.
Mexico—Emigration and immigration—History. I. Title. II. New immigrants
(Chelsea House)
E184.M5S37 2006
973'.046872—dc22   2006008380

Chelsea House books are available at special discounts when purchased in bulk quantities for businesses, associations, institutions, or sales promotions. Please call our Special Sales Department in New York at (212) 967-8800 or (800) 322-8755.

You can find Chelsea House on the World Wide Web at
http://www.chelseahouse.com

Series design by Erika K. Arroyo
Cover design by Takeshi Takahashi
Printed in the United States of America
Bang EJB 10 9 8 7 6 5 4 3 2 1

This book is printed on acid-free paper.

All links and Web addresses were checked and verified to be correct at the time of publication. Because of the dynamic nature of the Web, some addresses and links may have changed since publication and may no longer be valid.

Contents

Introduction

Robert D. Johnston

At the time of the publication of this series, there are few more pressing political issues in the country than immigration. Hundreds of thousands of immigrants are filling the streets of major U.S. cities to protect immigrant rights. And conflict in Congress has reached a boiling point, with members of the Senate and House fighting over the proper policy toward immigrants who have lived in the United States for years but who entered the country illegally.

Generally, Republicans and Democrats are split down partisan lines in a conflict of this sort. However, in this dispute, some otherwise conservative Republicans are taking a more liberal position on the immigration issue—precisely because of their own immigrant connections. For example, Pete Domenici, the longest-serving senator in the history of the state of New Mexico, recently told his colleagues about one of the most chilling days of his life.

In 1943, during World War II, the Federal Bureau of Investigation (FBI) set out to monitor U.S. citizens who had ties with Italy, Germany, and Japan. At the time, Domenici was 10 or 11 years old and living in Albuquerque, with his parents—Alda, the president of the local PTA, and Cherubino, an Italian-born grocer who already had become a U.S. citizen. Alda, who had arrived in the United States with her parents when she was three, thought she had her papers in order, but she found out otherwise when federal agents swept in and whisked her away—leaving young Pete in tears.

It turned out that Alda was an illegal immigrant. She was, however, clearly not a security threat, and the government released her on bond. Alda then quickly prepared the necessary paperwork and became a citizen. More than six decades later, her son decided to tell his influential colleagues Alda's story, because, he says, he wanted them to remember that "the sons and daughters of this century's illegal immigrants could end up in the Senate one day, too."[1]

Given the increasing ease of global travel, immigration is becoming a significant political issue throughout the world. Yet the United States remains in many ways the most receptive country toward immigrants that history has ever seen. The Statue of Liberty is still one of our nation's most important symbols.

A complex look at history, however, reveals that, despite the many success stories, there are many more sobering accounts like that of Pete Domenici. The United States has offered unparalleled opportunities to immigrants from Greece to Cuba, Thailand to Poland. Yet immigrants have consistently also suffered from persistent—and sometimes murderous—discrimination.

This series is designed to inform students of both the achievements and the hardships faced by some of the immigrant groups that have arrived in the United States since Congress passed the Immigration and Naturalization Services Act in 1965. The United States was built on the ingenuity and hard work of its nation's immigrants, and these new immigrants—primarily from Asia and

Latin America—have, over the last several decades, added their unique attributes to American culture.

Immigrants from the following countries are featured in THE NEW IMMIGRANTS series: India, Jamaica, Korea, Mexico, the Philippines, Ukraine, and Vietnam. Each book focuses on the present-day life of these ethnic groups—and not just in the United States, but in Canada as well. The books explore their culture, their success in various occupations, the economic hardships they face, and their political struggles. Yet all the authors in the series recognize that we cannot understand any of these groups without also coming to terms with their history—a history that involves not just their time in the United States, but also the lasting legacy of their homelands.

Mexican immigrants, along with their relatives and allies, have been the driving force behind the recent public defense of immigrant rights. Michael Schroeder explains how distinctive the situation of Mexican immigrants is, particularly given the fluid border between the United States and its southern neighbor. Indeed, not only is the border difficult to defend, but some Mexicans (and scholars) see it as an artificial barrier—the result of nineteenth-century imperialist conquest.

Vietnam is perhaps the one country outside of Mexico with the most visible recent connection to the history of the United States. One of the most significant consequences of our tragic war there was a flood of immigrants, most of whom had backed the losing side. Liz Sonneborn demonstrates how the historic conflicts over Communism in the Vietnamese homeland continue to play a role in the United States, more than three decades after the end of the "American" war.

In turn, Filipinos have also been forced out of their native land, but for them economic distress has been the primary cause. Jon Sterngass points out how immigration from the Philippines—as is the case with many Asian countries—reaches back much further in American history than is generally known, with the search for jobs a constant factor.

Koreans who have come to this country also demonstrate just how connected recent immigrants are to their "homelands" while forging a permanent new life in the United States. As Anne Soon Choi reveals, the history of twentieth-century Korea—due to Japanese occupation, division of the country after World War II, and the troubling power of dictators for much of postwar history—played a crucial role in shaping the culture of Korean Americans.

South Asians are, arguably, the greatest source of change in immigration to the United States since 1965. Padma Rangaswamy, an Indian-American scholar and activist, explores how the recent flow of Indians to this country has brought not only delicious food and colorful clothes, but also great technical expertise, as well as success in areas ranging from business to spelling bees.

Jamaican Americans are often best known for their music, as well as for other distinctive cultural traditions. Heather Horst and Andrew Garner show how these traditions can, in part, be traced to the complex and often bitter political rivalries within Jamaica—conflicts that continue to shape the lives of Jamaican immigrants.

Finally, the story of Ukrainian Americans helps us understand that even "white" immigrants suffered considerable hardship, and even discrimination in this land of opportunity. Still, the story that John Radzilowski portrays is largely one of achievement, particularly with the building of successful ethnic communities.

I would like to conclude by mentioning how proud I am to be the editor of this very important series. When I grew up in small-town Oregon during the 1970s, it was difficult to see that immigrants played much of a role in my "white bread" life. Even worse than that ignorance, however, were the lessons I learned from my relatives. They were unfortunately quite suspicious of all those they defined as "outsiders." Throughout his life, my grandfather believed that the Japanese who immigrated to his rural valley in central Oregon were helping Japan during World War II by collecting scrap from gum wrappers to make weapons. My uncles, who were also fruit growers, were openly hostile toward the Mexican immigrants without whom they could not have harvested their apples and pears.

Fortunately, like so many other Americans, the great waves of immigration since 1965 have taught me to completely rethink my conception of America. I live in Chicago, a block from Devon Avenue, one of the primary magnets of Indian and Pakistani immigrations in this country (Padma Rangaswamy mentions Devon in her fine book in this series on Indian Americans). Conversely, when my family and I lived in Storm Lake, Iowa, in the early 1990s, immigrants from Laos, Mexico, and Somalia were also decisively reshaping the face of that small town. Throughout America, we live in a new country—one not without problems, but one that is incredibly exciting and vibrant. I hope that this series helps you appreciate even more one of the most special qualities of the American heritage.

Note

1. Rachel L. Swarns, "An Immigration Debate Framed by Family Ties," *New York Times*, April 4, 2006.

Robert D. Johnston
Chicago, Illinois
April 2006

1

A Peaceful Warrior for Justice

Mexican Americans are the largest and fastest-growing immigrant group in the United States today. This book explores many fascinating aspects of this diverse and ever-changing group: their history and culture, their struggles and accomplishments, their contributions to society, and more. We begin our journey with the story of Rita and César Chávez—not because they were "typical" Mexican Americans, for there is no such thing—but because theirs is an important story, and one that offers valuable insights into the broader patterns of the Mexican-American experience.

THE FAMILY OF RITA AND CÉSAR CHÁVEZ

Rita Chávez was born in 1925, two years before her brother César. Their grandfather, whom they called Papa Chayo, had come to the United States in the 1880s. He had run away from a huge *hacienda*, or farm, in the state of Chihuahua in northern

Throughout his life, César Chávez—pictured here in 1966 at a press conference in San Francisco—fought for the rights of migrant American farmworkers. In 1962, Chávez cofounded the National Farm Workers Association (NFWA), a labor union that championed nonviolence and integrity in securing fair and equal working conditions for its members.

Mexico, where he had been treated like a slave. In 1909, he and his wife settled in a fertile valley along a branch of the Colorado River in Arizona, where they started a farm of their own.

Digging into the dry rocky earth with shovels and picks, they built irrigation ditches to water their crops. The farm prospered, providing plentiful food for their 15 children. One of their sons, Librado, married a woman named Juana Estrada, who also had come to Arizona from Chihuahua. Librado, Juana, and their family, which included Rita and César, grew corn, beans, squash, watermelon, and chili peppers. They also had horses, cows, and lots of chickens, and they ran a small grocery store. Running a farm is very hard work, so Rita and César always helped with the chores. They had a big extended family, with many aunts and uncles and nearly 200 cousins living nearby. Almost the whole area was full of the Chávez family.

Rita was very bright, and she loved school. When her brother César started going to school, the teachers would say, "Oh, you're Rita's brother,"[1] and say many nice things about her. César loved learning new things, but he was not very fond of school. For one thing, the teachers always made him speak English instead of Spanish, even on the playground. If he spoke Spanish, they would punish him by hitting his knuckles hard with a wooden ruler. Also, the other kids would make fun of him for being Mexican (in fact, he was an American citizen because he had been born in the United States). Sometimes they beat him up. He knew that bullying people for any reason was wrong, but he never fought back. His mother had taught him that "it takes two to fight," and it was a lesson he took to heart.

THE CHÁVEZ FAMILY LOSES ITS FARM

Rita's father, Librado Chávez, was very honest, and he trusted other people to be honest, too. He made a deal with a neighboring *Anglo*, or English-speaking white man, to clear out all the tree stumps from 80 acres of this neighbor's land. In exchange, Librado was supposed to receive 40 acres of land around the family's store. Day after day, month after month, working in the hot Arizona sun, Librado dug and pulled and dragged those stumps out of his neighbor's land.

When Librado finally finished this very hard work, he went to get the title to his 40 acres. He discovered that the land had already been sold to another Anglo. The whole deal was a trick. Librado was furious. He went to court to fight for that land, but his lawyer, also an Anglo, advised him to borrow money to buy the land. It was another trick. When the bill for the loan came due, Librado could not pay it. This was in 1937. The United States was in the middle of the Great Depression, and money and jobs were very scarce.

For the Chávez family, it was a terrible day. For 50 years, they had built that farm with only their own sweat and toil. Now it was gone. Like thousands of other people during the Great Depression, the Chávez family piled their few belongings into their car and headed west, leaving most of their extended family behind. People said that there was work in California.

FROM ARIZONA TO CALIFORNIA

The Chávez family arrived in California to find that it was not the land of opportunity they had heard about. Most of the good land was already owned by fruit and vegetable growers with huge farms, so the Chávezes had no choice but to work as migrant farm laborers. They went wherever they could find work, harvesting peas and walnuts here, planting broccoli and lettuce there, and living in shacks without electricity or running water or toilets. Sometimes they slept in a leaky tent in the muddy fields. Thousands of other families were desperate for work, so the growers could hire them for pennies a day.

These were very hard times for the Chávez family. Librado, Juana, and their five children worked from dawn to dusk under the hot sun, earning only a dollar or two. The work was backbreaking, because they had to stoop over all day long. Sometimes, if they were lucky, Rita, César, and the other children were able to go to school. César attended more than 30 different schools. With tremendous effort, he managed to graduate from the eighth grade.

CÉSAR EDUCATES HIMSELF

In 1944, César joined the navy. After World War II, he returned to California, married a woman named Helen Fabela, and began to raise a family. He also began to read many books, continuing his education on his own. He was especially interested in how poor people can make their lives better by working together. He read about Mahatma Gandhi, a small, peaceful man who became a towering figure in the struggle to make India independent from Great Britain. Gandhi taught that the struggle for justice had to be nonviolent, that violence would only breed more violence. César read about Saint Francis, who also preached nonviolence. The ideas of Saint Francis and Gandhi reminded César of Jesus Christ in the Bible and of the lessons he had learned from his mother: "It takes two to fight, and one can't do it alone."[2] He knew that if he used violence to struggle for justice, he would just end up with more violence and no justice.

César, a gentle, soft-spoken man, decided that he had to do something about the desperate conditions of the migrant farmworkers. A union, he thought, was the solution. A union is an organization in which all the workers speak with one voice, bargaining with the company not *individually* but *collectively*, so that the company cannot take advantage of individual workers (this is called "collective bargaining"). César thought that, if all the workers refused to work until they received fair wages, decent housing, and other things that they needed, then the growers would have to give in. The growers needed the workers. Without the workers, the crops would rot in the fields.

CÉSAR BEGINS TO ORGANIZE

In 1962, César began to organize migrant farmworkers. It was an uphill battle. Many had tried before, and all had failed. The workers were afraid to join a union or to go on strike. They were afraid that the growers would fire them, that they would lose their jobs, and that their children would go hungry. In the past, when the workers went on strike, the growers brought in replacement workers called "strikebreakers" or "scabs." The growers also hired thugs to beat up the strikers. The police, the courts, the judges, the state legislature, and the governor always sided with the growers, too.

Why? For one thing, the farmworkers did not have the right to unionize or bargain collectively like other workers. The Wagner Act, the 1935 law that granted workers the right to bargain collectively through their union and to go on strike, did not apply to migrant farmworkers. Also, the growers owned the land and made a lot of money selling all the crops the farmworkers planted, tended, and harvested. The growers' land, their money, and the fact that the law was on their side made them very, very powerful.

César was convinced that justice was on the side of the farmworkers. He drove his old car from one end of California to the other, talking to people in their homes, in the fields, wherever he found them. One by one, he convinced the migrant laborers to join the union. He got a lot of help from his brother Ricardo and his cousin Manuel, along with Dolores Huerta, Fred Ross, and others. In 1962, the union had its first big meeting in Fresno, California. They called their union the *National Farm Workers Association*, or NFWA. Their symbol was a black eagle on a red background, and their slogan was "*Si se puede*" ("Yes, we can!").

César's plan was to spend at least five years organizing the workers into the NFWA. Only when people were organized, he thought, would the union be powerful enough to force the growers to agree to fair contracts. This was during the same years that Dr. Martin Luther King, Jr., was struggling for the rights of African Americans. Dr. King also preached nonviolence in the fight for justice. The United States was slowly changing, and César knew that the farmworkers could win if they stayed true to their ideals.

THE FARM WORKERS' UNION

The first big strike came in 1965, before César thought that the workers were organized enough. He saw how committed they were, however, and he agreed to lead the strike. The union declared a strike against the farmers who grew grapes. How could he and the union know that the strike would last for five years?

In 1965, migrant farmworkers who worked in the grape fields of California went on strike in support of fair wages and decent housing. Led by NFWA president César Chávez, picketers such as this group outside a Safeway supermarket in Seattle, Washington, boycotted stores that sold California table grapes.

As the grapes began to rot on the vines and the growers began to bring in strikebreakers, the union came up with a great idea: a grape boycott. If the union could convince shoppers across the United States not to buy California grapes, then the grape growers would have to give in.

The NFWA tried everything it could to publicize the grape boycott. They marched hundreds of miles to Sacramento, California's capital, to petition the governor and legislature. They sent out mass mailings, advertised in newspapers and magazines, talked to reporters, and protested at grocery stores to ask customers not to buy grapes.

The dispute with the grape growers was bitter. Time and again, the police jailed César, Dolores Huerta, and other union leaders. The growers and their supporters harassed the striking workers, bullied and beat them, sprayed pesticides on them, and fired shotguns over their heads. The strikers never responded with violence. In 1968, César went on a hunger strike, refusing to eat for 25 days to protest the injustices and the growers' refusal to bargain fairly with the union.

Slowly, the boycott began to work. The grape growers were losing money. Meanwhile, people from all over the country flocked to California to support the farmworkers. Finally, in 1970, some of the grape growers signed contracts with the union. Soon, all the big growers had to sign on. After five years of great hardship and sacrifice, the strikers had won!

Grapes were just one product of dozens that farmworkers harvested, and conditions across California remained very bad. The grape boycott was followed by a lettuce boycott. In 1972, to show the world how bad things were, César went on a second hunger strike. He became so weak that people were afraid he would die. He survived, and three years later California passed a law that granted the farmworkers the right to organize and bargain through their union, now called the United Farm Workers of America. The struggle of the farmworkers continued through the rest of the 1970s and to the present day.

THE LEGACY OF CÉSAR AND RITA CHÁVEZ

César Chávez died in his sleep on April 23, 1993, at 66 years of age. He had devoted his life to improving the lives of Mexican-American farmworkers, asking nothing for himself. He died penniless, but with thousands of friends and admirers. More than 40,000 people came to his funeral. When César died, President Bill Clinton asked Americans to remember and honor his memory. César Chávez, the president declared, was "one of the great labor leaders of our time" who "taught us how injustice anywhere affects us everywhere."[3] The next year, President Clinton awarded him the Presidential Medal of Freedom, the highest civilian honor in the United States.

The memory of César Chávez lives on. There are many scholarship and award programs named after him, and hundreds of libraries, schools, parks, and streets across the country bear his name. In the year 2000, the state of California proclaimed March 31 César Chávez Day, a state holiday. Every year on March 31, thousands of people attend memorial services to honor the man and his struggle. Many consider him a true American hero, alongside Susan B. Anthony, Rosa Parks, Martin Luther King, Jr., and others who fought peacefully and selflessly to improve the lives of the poor and oppressed.[4]

What of Rita Chávez? After arriving in California at age 12, she worked for many years in the fields and canneries, in an electronics factory, and in several retail stores. In the 1970s, she went back to school, and, in 1980, at age 55, she graduated from high school. "People said I was too old to be in high school," she later recalled, "but it was my dream to get that diploma, and I did it!" As a child, she never made it past the seventh grade. In 2003, at age 78, she finally retired. When this book went to press, she was healthy and happy and living in San José, California, near her 6 children, 14 grandchildren, and 3 great-grandchildren. In the box on the following page, she recalls some of her experiences in the farm labor movement. *(continues on page 22)*

RITA CHÁVEZ MEDINA

The following firsthand account* of the National Farm Workers Association's (NFWA) and the Agricultural Worker's Organizing Committee's (AWOC) grape boycott is by Rita Chávez Medina, the sister of renowned labor leader César Chávez. Rita hosted the first meeting and would later serve as a notary public for the cause. In 1965, California grape pickers went on strike in support of higher wages and called for consumers not to purchase California grapes sold in supermarkets. The boycott lasted five years but led to the American agricultural industry's first industry-wide labor contract.

I remember that we hosted the first meeting for the grape boycott at our family's house in San José. One day César said to me, "Rita, there's going to be a big meeting at your house tonight; it's so we can get started on the grape boycott." I said, "Well, all right." And he said, "I won't be able to be there, I have some other business I have to take care of in Delano." I said, "OK, but then who's going to run the meeting?" He said, "You are, you're going to run the meeting." That's the way he was—he always had faith in me; he thought I could do anything. And if he thought I could do something, then I knew I could do it. He was always doing that [Laughter]! So we had the meeting in our house, 30 or 40 people came; there were teachers, preachers, city council members, students, farmworkers, all kinds of people—we had a very successful meeting.

Then I remember he said, "Rita, we need someplace to put all the things that people are donating for the grape boycott, so we're going to put them in your house and you'll be in charge of it all." So every week, my house filled up with things that people donated—food, clothes, shoes, blankets, money, all kinds of things. All week long, boxes and other things would come to our little house in San José and we'd stack them here and there. Then on Fridays, people would come and get them all, then it would start again the next day. That went on for a long time; our house was always filled with things the farmworkers needed because of the strike and the boycott.

During one meeting, someone said, "We really need a notary public** of our own, because we always have forms that need to be notarized." For several days after that, César said he was looking for a notary public. Then a few days later he came to the house with a big smile and he said to me, "I found a notary public!" I asked, "Who is it?" And he said, "You, Rita, you are our notary public!" I didn't think I could do it, but he told me I could, so I took some classes and filled out the paperwork and I became a notary public!

When we went on the long march from Delano to Sacramento, all those miles along the highway, I pushed my youngest child, Helen, in the stroller—she was just a baby then. Well, we marched so far that all the rubber wore away from the tires of that stroller. César said, "Oh, I'll buy you another one, don't worry about it." And I know he meant to [laughter].

I wasn't able to do a lot for the movement because I had small children at home, but I did what I could. I always did what César asked me to do. Usually he wouldn't even ask, he would just tell me in his gentle way, "Rita, this is what needs to be done, and you're going to do such-and-such," and since I knew it had to be done and he always had faith in me, I just went ahead and did it. That's how it was.

The most important thing to know about César is that whatever he did, he did from his heart. He really wanted to help the less fortunate. He gave so much of himself and his family. His family gave up a lot, too. His wife especially; his wife deserves a lot of credit, and the children, the whole family. Those were some very hard years, but some very good years. There are so many memories, I can't keep track of them all.

---

* Rita Chávez Medina, San José, California, telephone interview with the author, October 2005.

** A notary public is a person authorized to "notarize" a document, that is, to officially certify that the document is authentic (or real), usually done with an official seal and signature.

(continued from page 19)

In the early 1970s, César described his sister Rita: "She helped people with all kinds of complicated forms like immigration papers and applications for citizenship. Many still come to her now to make out their income taxes. What a tragedy that she was never able to go beyond the seventh grade. There is so much human potential wasted by poverty, so many children forced to quit school to go to work. Rita was one of thousands."[5]

César's remarks remain true today. There are millions of Mexican Americans just like Rita Chávez—people with the desire and the ability to succeed who are kept down by poverty and a lack of opportunity. The story of Mexican Americans' struggle for dignity and justice is long and fascinating. Parts are ugly and sad, full of injustice and brutality, and many more parts are hopeful and inspiring, filled with the very best of the human spirit. Despite the many obstacles that they have faced, and that they still face, Mexican Americans draw enormous strength from their culture, their families, their communities, and the promise of America as a land of opportunity and justice as they struggle to build better lives for themselves, for their children, and for their nation.

This book tells their story.

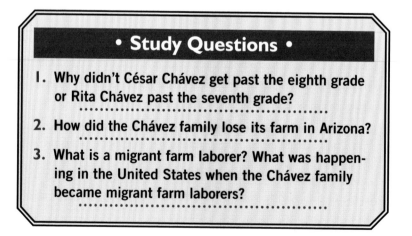

• Study Questions •

1. Why didn't César Chávez get past the eighth grade or Rita Chávez past the seventh grade?

2. How did the Chávez family lose its farm in Arizona?

3. What is a migrant farm laborer? What was happening in the United States when the Chávez family became migrant farm laborers?

4. What were conditions like for migrant farm laborers in California?
....

5. Why did César decide to try to form a union?
....

6. Why were the police, the courts, the governor, and the legislature on the side of the growers?
....

7. What are some ways to struggle without using violence?
....

8. What is a boycott? Why did the grape boycott succeed?
....

9. Is César Chávez really an American hero? Why or why not?
....

2

Border Crossings, 1800–1965

Snaking through rocky canyons, deserts, mountains, and cities from Brownsville, Texas, to San Diego, California, a 2,000-mile border separates Mexico from the United States—one of the longest land borders in the world. The border separates these two neighboring countries, but it also connects them. The histories and cultures of Mexico and the United States are bound together, like the tangled roots of neighboring trees.

In the mid-1840s, the border was far to the north of where it is now. Texas was then part of Mexico, as were California, Arizona, New Mexico, and parts of Colorado, Nevada, and Utah. In the Mexican-American War of 1846–1848, the United States conquered these lands and took them from Mexico. There is an old saying among longtime Mexican-American residents in the U.S. Southwest: "We never crossed the border; the border crossed us." How did this strange event come about?

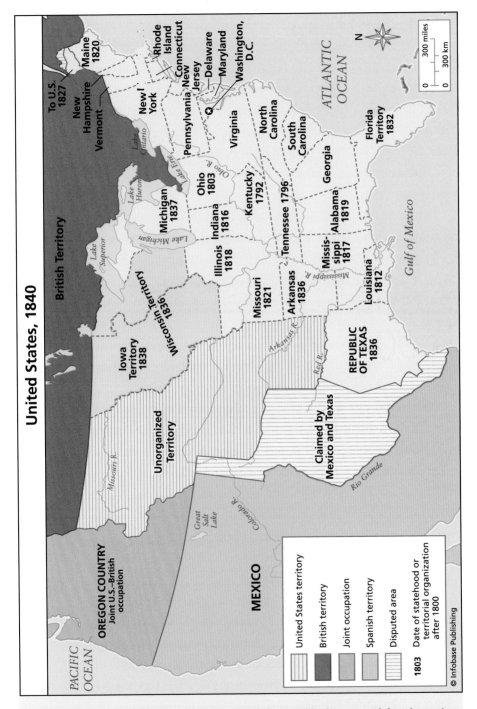

United States, 1840

British Territory

To U.S. 1827

Maine 1820

New Hampshire

Vermont

Rhode Island

Connecticut

New York

New Jersey

Pennsylvania

Delaware

Maryland

Washington, D.C.

Virginia

North Carolina

South Carolina

Georgia

Florida Territory 1832

Ohio 1803

Kentucky 1792

Tennessee 1796

Alabama 1819

Mississippi 1817

Michigan 1837

Indiana 1816

Illinois 1818

Missouri 1821

Arkansas 1836

Louisiana 1812

Iowa Territory 1838

Wisconsin Territory 1836

Unorganized Territory

REPUBLIC OF TEXAS 1836

Claimed by Mexico and Texas

MEXICO

OREGON COUNTRY Joint U.S.–British occupation

Lake Ontario

Lake Erie

Lake Huron

Lake Superior

Lake Michigan

Ohio R.

Mississippi R.

Arkansas R.

Red R.

Missouri R.

Colorado R.

Rio Grande

Great Salt Lake

PACIFIC OCEAN

ATLANTIC OCEAN

Gulf of Mexico

N

0   300 miles

0   300 km

Legend

| United States territory |
| British territory |
| Joint occupation |
| Spanish territory |
| Disputed area |

1803 Date of statehood or territorial organization after 1800

© Infobase Publishing

As depicted on this 1840 map of the United States, Mexico once claimed a vast area of the American Southwest that is today part of the United States.

THE EXPANSION OF COTTON AND SLAVERY

Before the 1820s, the people of the United States and Mexico had very little contact with each other. That began to change when landowners in the American South began to move west to find new lands to grow cotton. Planted and harvested by black slaves owned by Anglo-American plantation owners, cotton fetched a high price on world markets. Cotton rapidly depleted nutrients from the soil, though, so cotton growers were always looking for new and better lands. They were especially interested in the fertile soils of East Texas.

Beginning in the 1820s, thousands of Anglo-American farmers from the American South began to stream into East Texas to grow cotton and other crops, bringing their slaves with them. To them, it did not matter that Mexico claimed Texas. They were convinced that God favored white, English-speaking, Protestant men and women like themselves—that they had a right to own Texas. They also believed that the dark-skinned, Spanish-speaking, Catholic men and women of Mexico were inferior to them, just like their slaves, and so they ignored Mexico's claims.

The Mexicans who lived in these lands had many occupations. Some were storeowners and merchants, others blacksmiths and carpenters. Most earned their living from the land as farmers, ranchers, and cowboys (*vaqueros*). Despite what you may have seen in old Hollywood movies and TV shows—that almost all the cowboys in the old West were Anglos—in fact, the original cowboy was the Mexican vaquero.

THE LONE STAR REPUBLIC

In 1836, the Anglo-American settlers in Texas declared independence and founded a new country called "the Lone Star Republic." The Mexican government was furious. Determined to reclaim Texas, the government sent thousands of soldiers to fight the settlers. After many battles, including a famous one at a religious mission in San Antonio called the Alamo—where the

Texans lost—the Texans finally defeated the Mexicans. From 1836 to 1845, Texas was an independent country.

Meanwhile, many Anglo Americans wanted to make Texas and all the lands farther west part of the United States. They believed that Mexicans, like Africans and Indians, were inferior to them and should not stand in the way of what they thought was God's divine plan: a United States that stretched from the Atlantic Ocean to the Pacific. This idea was called "Manifest Destiny"—an idea that even the president of the United States strongly supported.

THE MEXICAN-AMERICAN WAR, 1846–1848

Mexico claimed all the land from Texas to California, so, in 1846, President James K. Polk asked the Senate to declare war on Mexico. The war raged until 1848, when Mexico conceded defeat. The Treaty of Guadalupe Hidalgo, which ended the war, granted the United States the northern two-fifths of Mexico. It was an enormous expanse of land, more than 529,000 square miles inhabited by 75,000 Mexicans and perhaps as many Native Americans. Manifest Destiny had become a reality. For the first time in its history, the United States stretched "from sea to shining sea."

Now you can see why some Mexican Americans in the border states say, "We never crossed the border, the border crossed us." In 1846, their ancestors were Mexican citizens. Two years later, living on the same plots of land, they were citizens of the United States.

SECOND-CLASS CITIZENS

At least the Treaty of Guadalupe Hidalgo *said* that they were citizens. Were they really? As you know, U.S. citizens have many rights—like freedom of speech and religion, the right to vote, and others—all the rights guaranteed by the Constitution, especially the Bill of Rights.

Were the Mexicans in these newly conquered lands really citizens? According to the treaty they were, but in practice they were not. In the decades after 1848, the Anglo Americans of Texas, California, and other conquered territories denied Mexican Americans the rights of citizenship. They denied them the right to vote through many clever means, such as poll taxes (making them pay a high tax before they could vote) and literacy tests (making them prove that they could read English). At the time, such tactics were perfectly legal. Those who resisted or demanded their rights were beaten, threatened, or even killed by gangs of gun-toting Anglos. One popular folk song in the Texas *borderlands* celebrates the memory of a local Mexican-American hero named Gregorio Cortez, who outsmarted these Anglo gangs time and again before they finally caught and jailed him.

Also, U.S. courts did not recognize Mexican-American deeds to the land—deeds written in Spanish and under Spanish law—so very often their lands were simply taken from them. In these and other ways, by the early 1900s, most Mexican Americans had been turned into second-class citizens—people who were supposed to enjoy all the precious rights of U.S. citizenship but who in practice had very few rights and were discriminated against by those who really held power.

"No Mexicans or Dogs"

Having lost their lands and their rights, many Mexican Americans became poor, low-wage laborers for the Anglo-American farmers, ranchers, and mine owners who dominated the American Southwest. Because anti-Mexican racism generally was very strong among Anglos, Mexicans were discriminated against in many ways, just as African Americans were. They could not testify in court against Anglos. They could not marry Anglos. They could not vote. They had to step off the sidewalk, take off their hats, and bow their heads when Anglos walked by. They had to obey signs outside restaurants, hotels, and other public places that read, "No Mexicans Allowed," and, "No Mexicans or Dogs." They were truly second-class citizens—yet they retained their language, their culture and values, and their hopes for a better future.

A GROWING MEXICAN-AMERICAN COMMUNITY, 1910–1930

Meanwhile, as you will see in the next chapter, Mexico was undergoing many changes. A handful of very rich people were coming to own most of the land, and most people were poor, owned no land, and were denied the most basic rights. In 1910, a vast social and cultural movement called the Mexican Revolution erupted. For the next 10 years, Mexico was engulfed in a massive civil war. More than a million people died. It was truly a horrific time.

Hoping to escape the violence and bloodshed, many Mexicans headed north to the United States. This was the first large movement of Mexicans across the border. From 1910 to 1920, roughly 250,000 Mexicans migrated to the United States. Most settled in Texas, New Mexico, Arizona, and California. Others moved farther north and east, to cities like Chicago, Detroit, Cleveland, and Pittsburgh. The years of the Mexican Revolution thus saw the birth of Mexican-American communities in many U.S. cities and towns.

This was also a time when the demand for labor in the United States was growing fast. World War I (1914–1918) began and ended while the Mexican Revolution was happening. During World War I, factory workers across the United States worked overtime to produce airplanes, guns, and many other war goods. Agriculture was also booming. Many farms from California to the Midwest and the Southeast grew fruits and vegetables—crops that had to be harvested quickly or they would rot. It was hard for farmers to find workers to harvest their crops at just the right time, so when Mexicans began to migrate north, these farmers saw a great opportunity. They hired Mexican migrants for the harvest season, paying them very low wages. Labor recruiters came to northern Mexico and border states like Texas and promised high wages and free transportation to the fields and orchards and back again. With few other opportunities, many signed on. When the season was over, the workers had to move on to harvest another crop somewhere else. In this way, many thousands of Mexicans and Mexican Americans became seasonal migrant laborers for American and Canadian fruit and vegetable growers.

There were two main migrant routes from Mexico: One followed California's Central Valley (where the Chávez family worked) and continued north into Washington State and British Columbia in Canada. Another followed the Mississippi and Ohio river valleys into the Great Lakes region, from Minnesota to Michigan and Ontario, Canada.

Following these seasonal migration paths, Mexican workers moved from field to field, most returning home when the work was done. Over the years, more and more decided to stay in the United States. Some settled in rural areas and small towns, others in big cities. Anyone born in the United States is automatically a U.S. citizen, and in this way, Mexican-American communities sprang up across the country. In the 1920s, an average of 50,000 Mexicans entered the United States each year. From 1920 to 1930, the Mexican-born population in the United States doubled, from 730,000 to 1.4 million (out of a total population of 123 million in 1930). By 1930, East Los Angeles was home to nearly 100,000 Mexicans, the biggest urban concentration of Mexicans outside of Mexico City. Thousands more lived in industrial cities in the Midwest such as Milwaukee, Wisconsin; Gary, Indiana; and Toledo, Ohio. The Mexican-American population was growing fast and spreading out across the country.

THE GREAT DEPRESSION, 1930–1940

This rapid growth came to a screeching halt with the onset of the Great Depression in 1930. As factories and mines closed and as middle-class and wealthy families fired their gardeners and maids, many thousands of Mexican Americans lost their jobs. The Depression hit farmers especially hard. When crop prices dropped and profits evaporated, many farmers left their lands untilled. Making matters worse was the Dust Bowl in the prairie states, where years of drought and overgrazing made millions

Number of Immigrants Admitted to the United States from Mexico, 1820–1960

Year of Entry	Number Admitted
1820	1
1821–1830	4,817
1831–1840	6,599
1841–1850	3,271
1851–1860	3,078
1861–1870	2,191
1871–1880	5,162
1881–1890	1,913
1891–1900	971
1901–1910	49,642
1911–1920	219,004
1921–1930	459,287
1931–1940	22,319
1941–1950	60,589
1951–1960	299,811

Source: Department of Homeland Security Web site. Available online at http://www.uscis.gov/graphics/shared/statistics/year-book/2004/table2.xls

of acres dry and barren. In both the city and countryside, hunger and homelessness grew. These were very hard times.

As the economy kept getting worse, many Anglo Americans blamed Mexicans for taking jobs that they thought should go to Anglos. States and communities across the country passed laws that required that Mexicans be deported back to Mexico—a process called *repatriation*. The federal government helped enforce these laws. From 1929 to 1934, more than 400,000 Mexicans and Mexican Americans were forcibly returned to Mexico. Many had been born in the United States, but their citizenship did not protect them. As a result, the steadily rising stream of immigration reversed itself. In the 1930s, more Mexicans migrated back to Mexico—or were forcibly repatriated—than entered the United States.

WORLD WAR II AND AFTERMATH, 1940–1965

World War II reversed the flow once again. The United States needed soldiers to fight the war against Germany and Japan, at the same time that the demand for labor in the nation's farms, factories, and mines soared. Nearly half a million Mexican Americans served their country in the armed forces. Thousands received medals and citations for bravery.

Official figures show 23,000 Mexicans admitted to the United States from 1941 to 1945. The actual numbers were much higher, because hundreds of thousands of undocumented workers migrated north. (*Undocumented* and *unauthorized* mean that they did not have the proper paperwork such as a passport or visa, as the law requires. Sometimes such unauthorized immigrants are called *illegal aliens*, an unfortunate term that makes them sound like outlaws from another planet.) Derisively called *wetbacks* by some Anglo Americans—their backs were supposedly wet because they swam across the Rio Grande—undocumented Mexicans proved vital to the U.S. war effort. Still, there were not enough workers to meet all of the economy's needs.

In response to this labor shortage, in 1942, the American and Mexican governments created the Bracero Program (*bracero* translates as "helping hand"). The agreement called for a certain number of Mexican agricultural workers (braceros) to enter the United States each year. When they completed their contracts, they would return to Mexico. The Bracero Program was meant to last only for the war years, but American farmers found the program so profitable that they convinced the government to extend it until 1965. Altogether, more than 5 million Mexicans worked as braceros. Having learned about the United States firsthand, many finished their contracts and returned as *undocumented migrants*. The abundance of braceros was one

In 1942, the Mexican and American governments created the Bracero Program, which called for a certain number of Mexican workers to be permitted to work in the United States each year. Pictured here are Mexican migrant workers harvesting crops on a California farm in 1964.

reason why it was so hard for migrant farmworkers to organize or strike successfully before 1965—because it was so easy for growers to find replacement workers. In many ways, the ending of the Bracero Program made it possible for César Chávez and the UFWA to launch a successful strike.

Some Americans thought that "illegal aliens" were taking jobs that should go to U.S. citizens. In 1954, the government launched "Operation Wetback" to rid the country of undocumented workers. Over the next 10 years, they deported millions of unauthorized Mexican immigrants. The 2,000-mile border proved too porous, however, and the forces pushing migrants out of Mexico and pulling them toward the United States too powerful. Despite tremendous obstacles, the undocumented migrants kept coming.

In 1965, the U.S. population stood at 190 million. About 10 to 15 million of these could claim Mexican ancestry. Clustering in the Southwest and spreading out to cities, towns, and rural areas across the country, they raised families, paid taxes, participated in civic life, and founded churches, unions, and other organizations. Mexican Americans were an increasingly vital and vibrant thread in the tapestry of the nation they called home.[6]

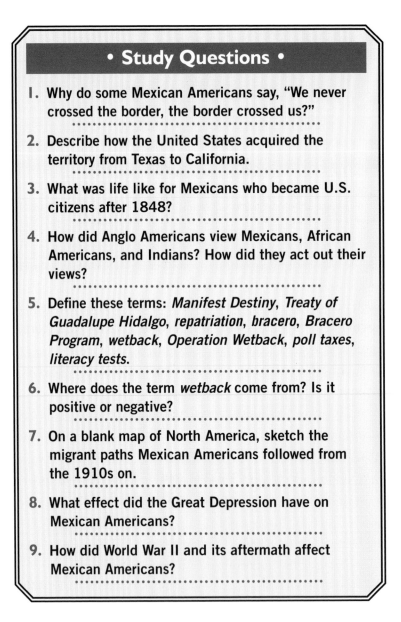

• Study Questions •

1. Why do some Mexican Americans say, "We never crossed the border, the border crossed us?"

2. Describe how the United States acquired the territory from Texas to California.

3. What was life like for Mexicans who became U.S. citizens after 1848?

4. How did Anglo Americans view Mexicans, African Americans, and Indians? How did they act out their views?

5. Define these terms: *Manifest Destiny, Treaty of Guadalupe Hidalgo, repatriation, bracero, Bracero Program, wetback, Operation Wetback, poll taxes, literacy tests.*

6. Where does the term *wetback* come from? Is it positive or negative?

7. On a blank map of North America, sketch the migrant paths Mexican Americans followed from the 1910s on.

8. What effect did the Great Depression have on Mexican Americans?

9. How did World War II and its aftermath affect Mexican Americans?

3

Homeland of the Children of Maize

The mountains and valleys of central and southern Mexico are home to some of the oldest civilizations on Earth. More than 3,000 years ago, the native peoples of this vast and rugged land began to build cities and towns; to grow crops such as *maize* (corn), beans, and squash; to create governments; and to form armies. Today, many traces of those ancient civilizations remain: the gigantic pyramids and plazas of Teotihuacán, the enormous stone heads carved by the Olmecs, the mysterious temples and stone-chiseled writings of the Maya, the many bits of ancient pottery that litter farmers' fields. When the Spanish arrived in the early 1500s, 25 million people lived in central and southern Mexico, heirs to cultures and civilizations that stretch back thousands of years.

THE CONQUEST OF MEXICO

The coming of the Spanish changed Mexico forever. In 1519, several hundred Spaniards invaded Mexico intent on discovering gold, conquering the inhabitants, and spreading their religion. At that time, the powerful Aztec Empire, ruled by people called the Mexica and founded less than 100 years before, dominated all of central and southern Mexico. Their capital city, Tenochtitlán, rose majestically from an island in Lake Texcoco, in the Valley of Mexico. Its skyline marked by massive temples and pyramids, the island city was home to 100,000 people. Peering down on it for the first time, the Spanish were astounded. They had never seen such a vast or well-ordered city.

Remarkably, these few hundred Spaniards swiftly conquered the mighty *Aztecs*. How was this possible? The Spaniards' guns, horses, superior military tactics, shrewd leadership, and sheer willpower accounted for some of the reasons. The Aztecs also had many local enemies who were eager to help the Spanish.

The center of the Aztec Empire, which ruled central and southern Mexico when the Spanish arrived in the early 1500s, was the city of Tenochtitlán. The city stood at the site of present-day Mexico City and was once home to approximately 400,000 residents—the largest residential concentration in Mesoamerican history.

However, the most important factor was the spread of European diseases, such as smallpox and measles. Native peoples had no biological immunity to the many deadly diseases that the Spanish unknowingly brought with them. For these and other reasons, in 1521, the Spanish defeated the Aztecs and reduced their magnificent city to rubble.

Despite everything you have just read, the fact remains that there were no Indians in Mexico before the Spanish conquest. "What?" you ask. "How can that be?" It is true. There were Aztecs, Tepanecs, Tlaxcalans, Cholulans, and many other groups, but none who called themselves "Indian." By the very fact of their conquest, the Spanish created the category of people called "Indian." It was a profound and lasting change.

COLONIAL NEW SPAIN, 1521–1821

Spain ruled Mexico for the next 300 years. Calling their colony New Spain, the Spaniards made the surviving Indians their servants and slaves and New Spain a source of riches for their kingdom across the sea. As the colony's silver and other treasures poured into Spain, slavery, violence, and diseases nearly wiped out the Indians. By the 1650s, fewer than one million survived—a population decline of more than 95 percent.

Meanwhile, as Spanish men mixed with Indian women, a new group appeared: *mestizos*, or "mixed-race" people. Class and race were like two sides of the same coin: The darker your skin, the poorer you were likely to be, and the lighter your skin, the wealthier. It was nearly impossible for people to improve their social positions: If you were born poor, you would very likely stay poor. Indians were at the bottom of society, mestizos in the middle, and the few "clean-blooded" Spaniards at the top. By the 1700s, Spaniards born in Mexico outnumbered those born in Spain and mestizos increasingly outnumbered both Spaniards and Indians.

Over time, a distinctly Mexican culture, combining Indian and Spanish cultures, emerged. Many Indian languages survived, as did many preconquest ways of working and living. Maize, beans, squash, chili peppers, and other native foods remained the colony's major crops. Women continued to make maize bread, or *tortillas*, just as their ancestors had for thousands of years.

To Indian peoples, maize was no ordinary crop. It was the Earth-Mother's most precious gift to her children, the lifeblood of her people, and it held a special place in spiritual life. The cultivation of maize originated in south-central Mexico thousands of years before, the result of centuries of careful selection of the best plants by many generations of native farmers. Their descendents, Indians and mestizos alike, were truly the children of maize.

The Spanish tried very hard to impose their religious beliefs on the conquered Indians, but they were only partly successful. Before the conquest, Indian peoples worshipped many gods— the sun god, the rain god, and others. After the conquest, Indians combined their own beliefs in many gods with the Christian belief in a single all-powerful God. Indian communities adopted patron saints like San Juan (Saint John), Santa María (Saint Mary), and many others, which they interpreted as new versions of their old gods. To this day, villages across Mexico celebrate their special saint's day with noisy processions, music and dance, and other festivities.

In 1531, just a few years after the conquest, an Indian named Juan Diego reported a miraculous vision of a dark-skinned virgin. This Virgin of Guadalupe became Mexico's most beloved patron saint and national symbol. Throughout Mexico, as in Mexican-American communities across the United States, her image can be seen almost everywhere.

Religion was one thing that held society together. The family, with the father at its head, was another. Then, as today, the male-dominated ("patriarchal") family was the colony's most basic institution. It was an unequal institution, because males held the most power. Men and fathers were expected to be strong, protective, and dominant over women and children. Women and mothers were expected to be nurturing and

In 1531, shortly after the Spanish conquest of Mexico, Juan Diego, a native convert to Roman Catholicism, reported having a vision of a dark-skinned Virgin Mary. Depicted in this painting by Mexican artist Pedro Antonio Fresquis (1749–1831), the Virgin of Guadalupe is Mexico's most beloved patron saint and a national symbol.

self-sacrificing and to obey their husbands and fathers. These gender roles, which many women found unfair, were called *machismo* (for men) and *marianismo* (for women).

Meanwhile, Spanish rule drained Mexico of its silver and other riches. In this once abundant land, there were poor people everywhere. A minority of landowners, priests, and government officials became wealthy, benefiting from the labor of the poor. The Catholic Church became the colony's largest landowner and its wealthiest and most powerful institution.

New Spain's rulers tried to govern the vast territory that they claimed, sending soldiers and missionaries to the northern frontier (what is now the U.S. Southwest) to establish missions and towns. In 1608, they founded Santa Fe, today the capital of New Mexico. (This was one year after the English colonists founded their first permanent settlement in North America at Jamestown in present-day Virginia.) Many Spaniards settled in the Upper Rio Grande valley—today in northern New Mexico and southern Colorado—where they mixed with local Indians. Years later, their descendents called themselves *hispanos*. By the late 1700s, Spain had established a string of missions from Texas to California. One, the Alamo, became famous in the Texas War for Independence.

Meanwhile, the 1700s saw great changes in Europe and North America. A major shift in thinking, called the Enlightenment, was encouraging people to question rule by king and church. In eastern North America, the 13 colonies of Great Britain debated independence and self-government. Their leaders discussed radical ideas like citizenship and democracy (rule by the people). In 1776, these 13 colonies declared independence and fought a revolution to win their freedom. In 1783, they became a new nation, the United States of America.

Many in New Spain also began to challenge Spanish rule. On September 16, 1810—celebrated as Mexican Independence Day—a Mexican-born Spanish priest named Miguel Hidalgo y Costilla rang the church bell in the little town of Dolores, gathered the townsfolk together, and cried out for independence. Soon, he led an army of 100,000 angry mestizos and Indians. The Spanish captured, tried, and beheaded him and dispersed his army. Others continued the struggle. In 1821, after 11 years of war, Mexico finally won its independence.

INDEPENDENT MEXICO

The new Republic of Mexico faced enormous challenges. The wars for independence had destroyed much of the economy. Most people remained poor and illiterate. Because there were few good roads, most rarely traveled far from home. All of this made the idea of a larger national community called "Mexico" hard for many to understand. Also, Mexico's leaders had different ideas about how the new country should be governed. The result of these and other conflicts was a series of unstable governments, dictatorships, and civil wars.

Another major source of problems came from foreign countries. Spain tried to reconquer Mexico in 1829. It failed, but other countries followed. France wanted to make Mexico part of its empire and did so in the 1860s, before the Mexicans defeated them. Before that, in the 1840s, the United States conquered the lands from Texas to California (see Chapter 2). Many Mexicans experienced this defeat as deeply humiliating and came to view the United States with a mixture of dislike, fear, and respect. They disliked the United States for taking their lands, and they feared more humiliation. They respected their neighbor's immense power, however, and sought to imitate it. These conflicting feelings toward the United States persisted. In the face of these outside enemies, the idea of Mexican national identity grew.

In the 1850s, after Mexico's defeat in the war with the United States, a new generation sought to reform and modernize Mexico. Their leader was Benito Juárez, sometimes called "Mexico's Abraham Lincoln." Good government proved elusive, however. After Juárez, a dictator named Porfirio Díaz ruled with an iron fist. His rule lasted from 1876 to 1910. Under Díaz, the poor grew poorer and the handful of rich became richer and came to own most of Mexico's land. Those who opposed Díaz were imprisoned or killed. Meanwhile, big U.S. companies came to control large parts of Mexico's economy, especially its rich mines of copper, silver, zinc, and tin.

Benito Juárez is sometimes referred to as "Mexico's Abraham Lincoln" for his efforts to modernize his country and resist French occupation. Juárez served two terms (1861–1863 and 1867–1872) as president of Mexico and his birthday (March 21) is a national holiday.

THE MEXICAN REVOLUTION

In 1910, a rebellion against Díaz was just the opportunity many had waited for. Revolts sprang up across the country. In the north, a colorful figure named Pancho Villa formed an army of thousands of unemployed miners and cowboys. In the south, a village leader named Emiliano Zapata led thousands of Indians with the cry "Land and Liberty!" The Mexican Revolution had begun.

For the next 10 years, from 1910 to 1920, Mexico was ablaze in revolution and civil war. More than one million people died, and a quarter million more migrated north across the border (see Chapter 2). In 1917, as the fighting raged, Mexicans adopted a new constitution, one that still governs the country today. The Constitution of 1917 guaranteed Mexicans many rights, including freedom of speech and religion and the right to bargain with employers. It granted men the right to vote (women were not granted the right to vote until 1955). It also tried to make the country's land ownership more equal, took away much of the Church's power, and forbade foreigners from owning Mexican land. This last provision angered the United States, especially its powerful mining and oil companies.

The Mexican Revolution and 1917 Constitution changed the country in important ways. Ordinary people were no longer afraid to speak out against the government, and many felt that they finally belonged to the Mexican nation. Soon, however, democratic rule was replaced. In the late 1920s, a new political party, the *Institutional Revolutionary Party* (PRI), came to dominate Mexican politics. For the next 70 years, the PRI won every presidential election. It became corrupt and dictatorial, ruling Mexico in a "one-party democracy" that even its leaders knew was not democratic.

FROM THE REVOLUTION TO THE PRESENT

Throughout the twentieth century, the Mexican economy became increasingly dependent on the U.S. economy. When the U.S. economy boomed, so did Mexico's. When the U.S. economy crashed, Mexico's crashed harder. This dependence increased in

1994 with the North American Free Trade Agreement (NAFTA) between Mexico, the United States, and Canada. Many argue that NAFTA favors American businesses like McDonald's, Coca-Cola, and Wal-Mart, whose low wages and cheap goods drive out smaller "mom-and-pop" Mexican businesses. Others disagree, arguing that NAFTA creates jobs and helps the economy. The debate about NAFTA continues.

Meanwhile, Mexico's population continued to climb. Its cities grew rapidly, especially after World War II. In 1900, fewer than 10 percent of all Mexicans lived in big cities. In 2000, about 75 percent did. People migrated to cities for many reasons, but mainly because cities offered more economic opportunities. Mexico City, the nation's capital, saw explosive growth. Today, it is home to nearly 25 million people—nearly one Mexican in four—making it the largest city in the Western Hemisphere, three times as big as New York City. In 2005, Mexico's population stood at 106 million, more than one-third of the U.S. population of 295 million.

THE ENGINE OF MIGRATION

Today, roughly 10 million Mexicans—nearly one in 10—live in the United States, the main destination of Mexican emigrants. Poverty remains the country's number one problem and the number one reason why so many decide to migrate north. Roughly half of all Mexicans live in poverty, and one-sixth live in extreme poverty. *Poverty* means living on about $4 per day, *extreme poverty* $2 per day. The average Mexican earns $6,300 per year, and the poorest half earns less than $1,700 per year. The average U.S. citizen earns $38,000 per year—six times more than the average Mexican and 22 times more than the poorest half of Mexicans.[7]

The arithmetic is simple, its consequences inescapable. As long as so many Mexicans remain so poor and as long as huge gaps in income and opportunity between Mexico and the

United States exist, Mexicans—a people whose history stretches back to the dawn of civilization—will continue to migrate north in search of a better life.

• Study Questions •

1. What made it possible for the Spanish to conquer the mighty Aztec Empire? Why did they?

2. In what sense were there no "Indians" in Mexico before the Spanish conquest? What happened to Mexico's Indians after the conquest?

3. Define these terms: *institutions, citizenship, democracy, national identity, race, class,* and *gender.*

4. What was the class structure like in New Spain? How were race and class related?

5. What were the main problems of independent Mexico?

6. How did Mexico change in the twentieth century?

7. What are the main factors prompting Mexicans to migrate north?

8. Why are Mexicans "the children of maize"?

9. Tell the adults in your family that you learned in one of your schoolbooks that there were no Indians in Mexico before the Spanish arrived. Write down their responses. Be patient. Don't explain it to them right away; give them a day or so to figure it out for themselves. Then tell them why it's true. Write down their responses again.

4

Across the Line

A DESERT TRAGEDY

It is early in the morning of April 6, 1996, in the southern California desert. The air is crisp and cool, the eastern sky glowing softly with the coming dawn. A blue pickup truck roars along a dusty road. Its cargo is so heavy that its fenders nearly scrape the tires. The truck carries 27 undocumented Mexicans, 2 in the front seat and 25 crammed into the camper in the back. Among them are Benjamín, Jaime, and Salvador Chávez, three brothers from the city of Cherán in the Mexican state of Michoacán.

A U.S. Border Patrol truck spots the blue pickup truck, which is obviously overloaded, and starts following it. The driver of the blue truck, a smuggler of undocumented Mexicans, or *coyote*, speeds away, his tires screeching with each turn in the road. Those crammed in the back, tossed around violently, start

A U.S. Border Patrol truck drives along the U.S.–Mexico border in Jacumba, California, east of San Diego. Part of the Department of Homeland Security, the U.S. Border Patrol has more than 9,500 agents who monitor the 2,000-mile border between Mexico and the United States.

to panic. They open the rear window and want to jump out, but they are going too fast. The blue truck zooms toward a sharp curve, and the driver swerves and loses control. The truck flies off the road, flips over in midair, and lands with a tremendous crash in the ditch.

The crash kills 8 people and injures 19, many critically. Among the dead are Benjamín, Jaime, and Salvador Chávez.

Three weeks later, far to the south, María Elena Chávez's eyes fill with tears. A small, thin woman in her mid-50s, she wears a traditional Indian *rebozo*, or embroidered shawl, draped over her shoulders. She lives in a humble shack in Cherán with her daughter Rosa; Rosa's husband, Wense; her son Fernando; and her seven grandchildren. Her heart is heavy with grief. She is the mother of Benjamín, Jaime, and Salvador, crushed to death in the California desert.

María Elena does not want her surviving children to go north across the border, to *the other side*. "I don't want another mother to suffer what I've suffered,"[8] she says softly. The town is very poor, however, and most of its families depend on the money sent to them by their sons and daughters in the United States—so those sons and daughters leave by the thousands, year after year. Many return in October for the annual fiesta of Saint Francis. They celebrate, spend time with their families, and enjoy being home. Then, come spring, they say their good-byes and head north again.

REMITTANCES FROM "THE OTHER SIDE"

The average worker in Cherán earns about $3 per day. Working in the United States, they can earn 20 or 30 times as much. It is no surprise that so many of the town's inhabitants—about one in three—migrate north to "the other side" each year. That is just in Cherán. In the state of Michoacán, where Cherán is located, nearly 3 million people make the journey north every year. In the spring and summer, some towns see their populations decline by two-thirds. In the fall, many return, bringing money, clothes, music, movies, televisions and DVD players, and other gifts for their families, friends, and sweethearts.

Most who undertake the journey are between 15 and 45 years of age, in the prime of their working lives. Most have no passport or visa. Instead, they hire "coyotes" to smuggle them across the border. Such workers, documented and not, bring or send about $5 billion per year to their families in Michoacán. That is three times more than the state of Michoacán spends in a year. Without these *remittances*, as the money sent back home is called, many families could not survive.[9]

Throughout Mexico, Central America, and the Caribbean, the story is much the same. In 2002, Mexicans working in the United States sent at least $10 billion to their families back home—an average of about $29 million per day. Most come in small amounts, $200 or less. Yet, just as millions of raindrops can cause a flood, these remittances have become Mexico's second-largest source of foreign exchange (money that comes in from outside the country). Remittances bring Mexico more money than tourism, more than farm exports, more than everything except oil. And they are growing fast.[10]

POLICING THE BORDER

It is also getting harder and harder for Mexicans to cross the border to live and work on "the other side." This is because the U.S. government, under pressure from anti-immigrant groups and lawmakers, keeps making it harder.

The U.S. Border Patrol (nicknamed *la migra* in Spanish) is the U.S. government agency charged with policing the border and keeping undocumented immigrants out of the country. Since the 1990s, the U.S. Border Patrol has paid special attention to places where the border separates big cities, especially San Diego/Tijuana, El Paso/Ciudad Juárez, and the two Nogaleses. They have hired more agents, bought more trucks, and begun to use special technologies, such as motion-activated video cameras and night-vision goggles, to spot people sneaking across the border. They also started to build a huge fence between San Diego and Tijuana, which are so close that they almost form one giant city. The fence, still incomplete, stretches for miles into the desert. More and more Mexicans have traveled deeper and deeper into the desert—a harsh, fearsome, unforgiving place of blistering heat and bitter cold, of gnawing hunger and blinding thirst—to cross to "the other side." As a result, more are dying.[11]

In 1996, the Mexican government reported that 87 Mexicans had died trying to cross the border. Three were named Benjamín, Jaime, and Salvador Chávez. In 2000, the number rose to 376—more than four times as many. The number is still rising. Especially since the terrorist attacks of September

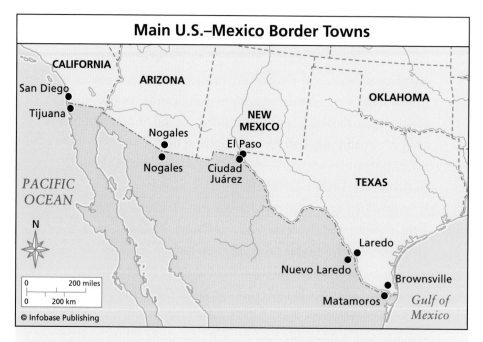

Main U.S.–Mexico Border Towns

CALIFORNIA

ARIZONA

San Diego

Tijuana

OKLAHOMA

NEW MEXICO

Nogales

El Paso

Nogales

Ciudad Juárez

TEXAS

PACIFIC OCEAN

N

Laredo

Nuevo Laredo

Brownsville

Matamoros

Gulf of Mexico

0   200 miles

0   200 km

© Infobase Publishing

Many illegal immigrants attempt to cross into the United States at one of five locations where major cities straddle each side of the border. In these areas— San Diego/Tijuana, El Paso/Ciudad Juárez, Laredo/Nuevo Laredo, Brownsville/ Matamoros, and the two Nogaleses—the U.S. Border Patrol has hired more agents, bought more trucks, and begun to use special technologies to curtail illegal crossings.

11, 2001, the U.S. government has tightened security along the border even more. The early 2000s saw a growing number of horror stories of failed efforts to "cross the line." In October 2002, railroad workers in Denison, Iowa, opened up a locked boxcar from Matamoros, Mexico, and found the skeletons of 11 undocumented Mexicans. They had become trapped in the boxcar and died.[12] A few months later, near Victoria, Texas, police discovered an abandoned truck-trailer crammed with perhaps as many as 100 men, women, and children from Mexico and Central America, all undocumented workers. Among them were 19 dead, including a five-year-old boy—victims of dehydration, extreme heat, and suffocation. The coyote later pled guilty to causing 19 deaths. Such stories are becoming increasingly common.[13]

In short, crossing the border illegally can be very difficult and very dangerous. It is also expensive, $1,000 or more, to hire a coyote, with no guarantee of success—yet millions keep trying, and most succeed. Many return, year after year. Others decide to stay.

THE FIRST GENERATION: THE STORY OF CARLOS FERNÁNDEZ

People born in other countries who settle permanently in the United States are called "first-generation immigrants." A good example of a first-generation immigrant is Carlos Fernández, born in Chihuahua City in 1938. At age 11, he came to the United States with his brother. "The first time I came, I worked picking cotton, which was very difficult,"[14] he recalled of his youth. "Later, I worked in nearly every type of agricultural job there was: beets, tomatoes, lettuce, pecans, apples, pears."[15] As a teenager, he worked on shrimp boats off Texas and in the orange groves of Florida. Then he went north to New England, where he worked in Connecticut for a tobacco company, and in Massachusetts, New Jersey, and many other places.

In New England, Carlos made friends with some Puerto Ricans, a group granted U.S. citizenship in 1917 (because the United States controlled Puerto Rico and because of the need for soldiers in World War I). He pretended to be Puerto Rican. "Since I didn't have any papers and I looked Puerto Rican because of my curly hair, I had no problem getting jobs. I learned to speak like they did, and I never had any trouble with the *migra*."[16] In the 1950s, he returned to Florida, met a young Mexican-American woman from Michigan, and married.

Mexican Immigrants Admitted Under Different Preference Categories, 1998 to 2004

Year	Total	Family-sponsored preferences	Employment-based preferences	Immediate relatives of U.S. citizens (Total)	Spouses of U.S. citizens	Children	Parents
2004	175,364	64,463	7,225	99,718	59,052	17,941	22,725
2003	115,864	29,664	3,261	78,782	42,990	14,954	20,838
2002	219,380	58,602	7,492	150,693	93,968	25,103	31,622
2001	206,426	73,738	7,291	122,496	71,752	25,841	24,903
2000	173,919	77,857	3,950	88,997	47,281	20,808	20,908
1999	147,573	69,781	2,637	70,637	32,259	15,134	23,064
1998	131,575	55,140	3,586	71,731	38,548	15,954	17,229

Source: Department of Homeland Security Web site. Available online at http://www.uscis.gov/graphics/shared/statistics/yearbook/2004/table8.xls

"When my wife was expecting our first child, I went to get the doctor, but no one would come because at that time they did not see hispanos [*Hispanics*]. . . . Our daughter was born in

Pennsylvania, in the migrant camp. . . . Times were very difficult for us then."[17]

He and his wife worked very hard as they raised their two children. Years later, he felt very proud of his children's accomplishments—and of his own.

> When I married, I had nothing, absolutely nothing, nada, nada, nada. . . . If you could have seen me when I started out, and look at me now, you would know that I have come a long way. My daughter graduated from one of the best schools in the U.S. . . . and my son is studying electronic engineering at the university. . . . If you want to measure how far I have come, you have to know where I began. No one has ever given me anything. And there are many people like myself. [18]

His children's education was especially important to him, as were a strong sense of community—in his neighborhood, his church, and his workplace—and a sense of dignity and self-worth, for himself and for all Mexican Americans.

> Mexican people recognize their worth now, they have more self-respect. It's a fundamental change. . . . It's the environment we live in that has made us believe that we are equal. We value ourselves more because our children go to school, they see that the American believes in equal rights, and they realize that this includes them, too. This is one reason why education is so important for the future of our people. . . . It's like working on a precious stone. You don't notice the work that you've done while you're doing it, but later you see the beautiful results. That's the lesson that the Mexican kid is learning in school—that he is equal to all the rest—and because of that he not only stands up for his rights, but he also respects himself.[19]

Carlos Fernández is an example of a first-generation Mexican immigrant who, in the face of tremendous obstacles and hardships, created a successful life in the United States. Such first-generation immigrants often start a "chain" of immigration that can last for generations.

CHAIN MIGRATION: THE TAPIA FAMILY AND WARREN, ARKANSAS

Generally, immigration works as a two-step process: First-generation immigrants like Carlos Fernández settle in a new place, after which other family members and friends follow. This is called "chain migration," with the first immigrant, or "pioneer," being the first link in the chain. A good example can be found in the little town of Warren, Arkansas (population 6,500). In 1968, Raúl Tapia was picking grapes in California when he heard a rumor about a tomato farm in Warren. He traveled to Warren and worked harvesting tomatoes. He liked it. The boss seemed fair, and the hills and pine trees reminded him of his home in Cherán, Michoacán (he was a neighbor of Maria Elena Chávez and her family).

When the 1968 tomato picking season ended, Raúl Tapia left Warren. Over the next few years, he kept thinking about the town's lovely pine trees and decent bosses. Nearly 20 years later, he and his wife, Yolanda, decided to move their family there permanently. They became one of Warren's first, or "pioneer," Mexican families. Raúl got a good-paying job with the town's public works department. Over the next few years, more and more friends and neighbors followed. By the early 2000s, there were perhaps 60 Mexican families in Warren—most from Cherán—making up about 10 percent of the town's population, and their numbers were growing. Raúl Tapia's five children, second-generation Mexican Americans, have all gone on to college.[20]

Not all second-generation immigrants are as successful as the Tapia children. Many struggle to overcome poverty and discrimination. Such is the case with one of Mexican-American poet and author Sandra Cisneros's fictional characters.

Between the Generations

PATRICIA PRECIADO MARTIN RECOUNTS HER FAMILY'S INFLUENCE

Patricia Preciado Martin (b. 1937) is a prizewinning Mexican-American author who spent most of her life in southern Arizona. She has written many stories and books, including "The Legend of the Bellringer of San Agustín," a bilingual children's story (1980), and *Songs My Mother Sang To Me: An Oral History of Mexican American Women* (1992). Her many awards and honors include Arizona Author of the Year (1997) and the Arizona Humanities Council's Distinguished Public Scholar Award of Excellence (2000). In this passage, she describes the role that history, memory, family, and place have played in her life and work.

My memories of growing up Mexicana are very powerful and have been a strong influence as well as a source of inspiration for my writing. We lived in a small mining community south of Tucson for a few years, and the desert and open spaces were my playground. This instilled in me a love of nature and the land. We lived with my grandmother in Barrio Hollywood for a couple of years, and the images there are still very vivid in my mind—my abuelita's [grandmother's] garden, the raspada vendor [snow cone seller], the family gatherings, the devotion of my grandmother to her santos [saints]. The stories of my grandfather's ranch in Mexico became a mini-legend in my family and explain for me my strong ties to the land. My mother was a great influence on my life—education was most important to her. We are a very close family—this strong sense of familia [family] comes from our growing-up years—the required Sunday visits to my abuelita who didn't speak English. I am proud of my rich culture; it has made my life varied, interesting, and full.*

---

*Editor's introduction to "The Ruins" by Patricia Preciado Martin, in *Growing Up Chicana/o*, edited by Tiffany Ana López (New York: Avon Books, 1993), 25–26.

THE SECOND GENERATION: THE STORY OF ESPERANZA CORDERO

In her wonderful novel *The House on Mango Street*, Sandra Cisneros tells of a young girl named Esperanza Cordero. Esperanza lives in Chicago. She learns English at school, but her parents speak Spanish at home. In her neighborhood live Mexicans, Puerto Ricans, and other Latinos, all "brown" like her. Esperanza is American through and through, yet her family's roots reach deep into Mexico. Family, community, church, music, food, language—all these and more have a strongly Mexican flavor.

Esperanza's family is poor. They live in a house on Mango Street, "small and red with tight steps in front and windows so small you'd think they were holding their breath."[21] The whole family—Esperanza, her three siblings, and her mother and father—sleeps in the house's one bedroom. The city, like the house, feels dirty and crowded. "You can never have too much sky," she feels, but in the city, "there is too much sadness and not enough sky."[22]

Esperanza feels frustrated at her family's cramped house and poverty, at the grit and grime of the city, but she accepts it as part of life. She feels bad about the racial discrimination people in her neighborhood face when they go to other parts of the city. "All brown all around, we are safe. But watch us drive into a neighborhood of another color and our knees go shakity-shake and our car windows get rolled up tight and our eyes look straight."[23] Going outside of her neighborhood can be scary, but within it she feels comfortable and safe, surrounded by friends and families she knows.

She feels especially frustrated at being a girl, because girls have so few opportunities. Boys have much more freedom and power, she feels. Girls are expected to marry young, have lots of babies, stay at home, and obey their husbands. "Mexicans," she believes, "don't like their women strong."[24] Esperanza wants more from life. She aches for more freedom and opportunities,

In her 1991 novel *The House on Mango Street*, Sandra Cisneros (pictured here) recounts the story of Esperanza Cordero, a young Mexican-American girl who lives in Chicago. Esperanza, which means "hope" in Spanish, is proud of her Mexican heritage but dreams of one day escaping the poverty of her neighborhood.

but she feels like "a red balloon, a balloon tied to an anchor."[25] She wants to fly free, like a balloon soaring high in the sky, but she is not sure how to untie herself from the anchor of being a Mexican-American girl growing up on Mango Street. It is very hard.

Yet she loves her family and friends very much, and she is proud to be Mexican American. In Spanish, *esperanza* means "hope," and the verb *esperar* means both "to hope" and "to wait." This might be the author's way of expressing a common experience among second-generation Mexican Americans like Esperanza Cordero: how they wait and hope for a better future.

A SENSE OF COMMUNITY: DETROIT'S COLONIA MEXICANA

One of the major themes in *The House on Mango Street* is the strong sense of community felt by Esperanza and others in her Chicago neighborhood. In this way, at least, her fictional neighborhood is not unique. Just about everywhere that Mexican Americans have settled, a strong sense of community has developed—especially since the 1960s and 1970s, when Mexican Americans began to feel renewed pride in their culture and heritage.

Detroit's Mexican-American neighborhoods, called the *Colonia Mexicana*, are a good example. Mexicans began to settle in the Detroit area in the 1910s. By the late 1920s, the city had nearly 15,000 Mexican residents. Many came from Michigan's sugar beet fields to work in the fast-growing automobile and steel industries. Others opened grocery stores, restaurants, and shops. They did not settle in one area but rather clustered in three sections west of downtown.

During the Great Depression, as jobs disappeared and repatriations grew, Detroit's Mexican population declined sharply. By the late 1930s, only about 1,000 remained, scattered in different parts of the city. "They [were] completely

Americanized,"[26] recalled one longtime Mexican-American resident. This was common from the 1930s to the 1950s, as racial discrimination, fears of deportation, and pressures to "fit in" encouraged many to hide their Mexican ancestry (much the same as Carlos Fernández, who pretended to be Puerto Rican while he worked in New England).

Still, Mexican culture and community life endured. The 1960s and 1970s saw a flowering of cultural pride among Detroit's Mexican Americans, a flowering that continues today. Three special holidays in particular bring the community together: the Day of the Dead celebrations (November 1 and 2), sort of like Halloween, with skeletons and ghosts and other scary stuff; the Fiestas Guadalupanas (December 12), celebrating the Virgin of Guadalupe; and the Christmas celebration called "Las Posadas" (December 16 to 24), which reenacts the story of the birth of Jesus. These colorful celebrations are both solemn and joyous and include street processions, religious services, storytelling, theatre, music, dance, games—and, of course, mountains and mountains of delicious, mouthwatering Mexican foods.

Such celebrations have helped members of Detroit's Mexican-American community create a feeling of shared identity and pride in their heritage and culture. As community activist María Guadalupe Aguirre declared, "I teach my children to be proud of being Mexican. . . . We are the lucky ones here, for we have two cultures."[27]

Across the country, just as in Detroit, a shared history and culture has helped foster a strong sense of community and common identity among Mexican Americans. Does this mean that Mexican-American communities have no divisions or conflicts? Of course not—no community is conflict free. Among the most common conflicts are those between richer and poorer members of the community, between those who emphasize their Mexican heritage and those who do not, between recent arrivals and longtime residents, between males who want to dominate females and females who want gender equality, and between older and younger generations.

Despite these divisions, many Mexican Americans find deep satisfaction in feeling like part of a larger group, a feeling many seek to build on as they look to the future. From San Diego to New York and beyond, despite the many dangers and hardships of trekking north "across the line," it is a community that powerful forces are making bigger every day.

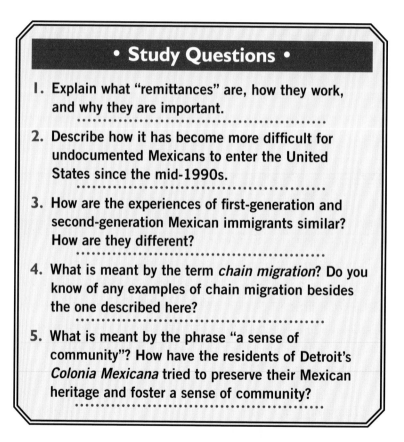

• Study Questions •

1. Explain what "remittances" are, how they work, and why they are important.

2. Describe how it has become more difficult for undocumented Mexicans to enter the United States since the mid-1990s.

3. How are the experiences of first-generation and second-generation Mexican immigrants similar? How are they different?

4. What is meant by the term *chain migration*? Do you know of any examples of chain migration besides the one described here?

5. What is meant by the phrase "a sense of community"? How have the residents of Detroit's *Colonia Mexicana* tried to preserve their Mexican heritage and foster a sense of community?

5

MexAmerica

A DEMOGRAPHIC EARTHQUAKE

Sometime in 2001—no one knows exactly when—a massive earthquake struck the United States. It did not knock down any buildings or shatter any windows. It did not even shake the ground. It was a *demographic* earthquake (demography is the study of populations, their characteristics, and changes over time). Sometime in 2001, Hispanics surpassed African Americans to become the country's largest minority group.[28]

That may not seem very important, but in fact it represents a monumental change. Since the early 1600s, when English colonists first began to settle in North America, Native American Indians and, later, African Americans were the largest minority groups. That continued for nearly 400 years—until 2001.

It was, therefore, a major historical event when Hispanics became the nation's largest minority group (on top of being its

Number of Immigrants Admitted to the United States from Mexico, 1961–2004

Year of Entry	Number Admitted
1961–1970	453,937
1971–1980	640,294
1981–1990	1,655,843
1991–2000	2,249,421
2001–2004	710,810
Total number admitted since 1961	**5,710,305**

Source: Department of Homeland Security Web site. Available online at *http://www.uscis.gov/graphics/shared/statistics/year-book/2004/table2.xls*

fastest-growing, which they had been for decades). But what is a *Hispanic?* There is no simple answer to this question. Not everyone agrees on what the term means, and not everyone uses it. Indeed, many so-called "Hispanics" prefer to be called *Latinos,* which is the term used here.

According to the U.S. Census Bureau's definition, "Hispanics" are people of any race who can trace their ancestry to Spain or Latin America. It thus includes Spanish Americans, Cuban Americans, Dominican Americans, and many other groups—including, of course, Mexican Americans.

Of all Latino groups in the United States today, Mexican Americans are the largest by far—two-thirds of the total. In 2000, according to the U.S. Census Bureau, there were 281 million people in the United States. Of these, 35 million were Latinos, including 21 million Mexican Americans. Latinos were thus 12.5 percent of the total population—one person in eight. (Mexican Americans made up 59 percent of all Latinos and 7.4 percent of the total population.)

"Wait a minute," you say. "A second ago you said that, in 2000, Mexican Americans were two-thirds of all Latinos. Now you say they were 59 percent. Which is it?" The problem is that the U.S. Census Bureau counts only legal immigrants. Millions of Mexican immigrants are not legally authorized, and many thousands arrive and depart each year depending on the seasons, the job market, and other factors. There are also thousands of "legal temporary migrants," like the braceros, who are not considered "immigrants." There are actually *four* categories of Mexican-born people in the United States: (1) U.S. citizens, (2) legal permanent residents, (3) legal temporary migrants, and (4) undocumented (im)migrants.

The U.S. Census Bureau counts only the first two categories, so its numbers are too low (as you can see, figuring out the actual number of immigrants is complicated). The best estimates are that about 5 million unauthorized Mexicans lived in the United States in 2003 and that about half a million more have arrived each year since. The actual number of Mexicans and Mexican Americans in the United States in 2006 is probably 25 to 30 million—about 9 to 11 percent of the total population—although no one knows for sure. One thing everyone agrees on: Their numbers are growing fast.

A GROWING SLICE OF AN EXPANDING PIE

How fast? By the year 2050, Latinos are expected to make up one-fourth of the total U.S. population. Perhaps two-thirds of those will be of Mexican ancestry.

Here is another way to think about it: Imagine the total U.S. population today as a pumpkin pie. Cut that pumpkin pie into eight equal slices. One of those eight slices represents all Latinos in the United States today—call it the Latino slice. Another slice is African Americans. Six slices remain. Five-and-a-half of those are European Americans (whites). The remaining half-slice is divided among Asian Americans, Native American Indians, Pacific Islanders, and other groups. Now, take the Latino slice—one-eighth of the pie—and cut it into three equal chunks. Two of those chunks are people of Mexican ancestry.

Now, imagine the future. You are in your 20s, your 30s, your 40s. Each year that passes, the pie grows bigger (the total population rises), and each year, the Latino portion of the pie grows larger. By the year 2050, Latinos will be at least two slices (one-quarter of the pie). African Americans will be about a slice-and-a-quarter (about one-seventh); Euro-Americans about four slices (half); and Asian Americans and all other groups about

HISPANIC? LATINO? WHAT'S IN A NAME?

There is considerable confusion and controversy about the labels applied to people of Latin-American origin living in the United States. The two most common labels are "Hispanic" and "Latino." Where do these labels come from, and what do they mean?

The root of the word *Hispanic* is *España*, which means *Spain* (actually Spain and Portugal, which together make up the Iberian Peninsula, or Iberia). Technically, then, *Hispanic* refers to people who can trace their ancestry to Spain (or Iberia), which is a *place*. The problem is that it excludes people who have no Spanish or Iberian ancestors at all—for example, Indians from Mexico, Bolivia, and elsewhere; Afro-Cubans and Afro-Dominicans; and many others. That is why some reject the term *Hispanic*—because it leaves out so many people.

The root of the word *Latino*, on the other hand, is "Latin," which is a *language*. It therefore refers to people who trace their ancestry to speakers of Latin-based languages, especially Spanish and Portuguese. Because the great majority of Latin Americans, including most people of Indian and African ancestry, speak three-quarters of a slice. Of course, all these numbers are projections from current trends, so no one really knows.

People describe this growing Latino population in different ways. Mostly they use images and metaphors having to do with water: a "rising tide," a "flood," a "torrent" of immigrants "pouring in" to the country. These are vivid images, but they can also make it seem like all these Latinos "streaming" and "flooding" into the country are going to drown everybody else. That is not a very helpful way to look at it, because rising floodwaters sound threatening and scary. Who wants to drown? If a "flood" of immigrants is indeed "pouring in," the solution would seem to be to dam the streams or raise the levees. In the case of the United States and Mexico, that

either Spanish or Portuguese, many people consider "Latino" more inclusive and for this reason prefer "Latino" to "Hispanic."

Some critics argue that neither label is appropriate because both lump together people of incredibly diverse origins and backgrounds, from wealthy light-skinned Cuban doctors in Miami to impoverished dark-skinned Ecuadorian factory workers in North Carolina. Still others argue that Hispanics/Latinos have a shared interest in having a common label because it can help them get minority scholarships; government contracts targeted to minority groups; greater political representation in local, state, and federal governments; and other benefits.

The controversy between these and other labels continues, and in the end there is no perfect term on which everyone agrees. What to do? One solution would be to ask people what they call themselves and what they prefer to be called and then respect their decision.*

* For further discussion, see Suzanne Oboler, *Ethnic Labels, Latino Lives* (Minneapolis: University of Minnesota Press, 1995).

In 2001, Latinos surpassed African Americans to become the largest minority group in the United States. Pictured here are people walking down a street in central Los Angeles's Westlake district. The Southern California city has the nation's largest population of Mexican Americans.

would mean tightening border security. One of the most important questions facing the United States today is whether or not this is a good idea.

A MELTING POT, A SALAD BOWL, A QUILT, OR NONE OF THE ABOVE?

The United States prides itself as being a "nation of immigrants," a nation that draws its strength from its tremendous ethnic, racial, and cultural diversity. The classic metaphor is the "melting pot." Immigrants from around the world come to America's shores and jump into the pot. The pot boils, the ingredients blend, and *voilà!*—Americans! The basic idea behind the melting pot is a bit different from the idea of assimilation, in which minority groups become similar to or are absorbed by the majority group (this idea is called "Anglo conformity").

This "melting pot" image works fairly well for Euro-Americans, or what Americans call "white" people—although it is also interesting to learn how different groups *became* "white" over time, like the Irish, Italians, and Poles, who from the 1800s to the early 1900s were not considered completely "white." What about "nonwhite" groups? Here the melting pot concept does a poor job of describing the actual relationships between whites and nonwhites.

Faced with the weaknesses of the melting pot concept, people came up with a different image: that of the salad bowl. In a salad, chunks of green peppers do not blend into the pieces of lettuce, which do not melt into the chunks of tomato, and so on. Everything pretty much stays as it is. They also came up with the idea of the quilt: a bunch of swatches of cloth stitched to each other (each piece representing an ethnic group), until there is a big patchwork quilt or mosaic.

Are these helpful metaphors? In some ways yes, in other ways no. Ethnic groups and cultures do not totally blend into each other; nor do they stay exactly as they are. They influence each other, with lots of "borrowing" among them, yet they

A group of illegal immigrants jumps a fence separating the
United States and Mexico. The U.S. Senate passed a bill
in April 2006 that is slated to provide more money to pay
for new U.S. Border Patrol agents, aircraft, and additional
fencing between the two countries.

also retain many of their own features. You can probably think of many examples in your own background. That is a big weakness of the quilt and salad bowl metaphors: The boundaries between the pieces are too firm and fixed. The main weakness of the melting pot idea is the opposite: The groups lose their individuality and dissolve into one big mixture.

Perhaps the biggest weakness of all these ideas is that they ignore that some groups have more power than other groups. We saw this in the Southwest after the Treaty of Guadalupe Hidalgo. Who had power then? Who had power under slavery? Where is the idea of power, especially the greater power of white people, in the melting pot, the salad bowl, or the quilt? It is just not there. It seems that none of these images really capture the American historical experience. Still, each can help us understand part of the process. Because of that, they are important images to keep in mind.

These images also have a common strength. All, in different ways, support the argument that America's real strength comes from the diversity of its peoples and cultures. This is a powerful and important argument, one that the author happens to agree with, although not everyone does. (You do not have to agree with it, either. What you do need to do is to figure it out for yourself. That is what an educated citizen in a democracy is supposed to do.)

As you have seen, from the mid-1800s to the present, Latinos have become an increasingly important part of the nation's diverse population. Their rapidly growing numbers in recent years represent only the latest stage in a very long process. That is part of an even bigger process, one that all of these images of melting pots and salad bowls are trying to describe: how different groups in the United States have struggled to recreate and reinvent a sense of what it means to be an American.

MEXICAN CANADIANS

What about Canada? Like the United States, Canada is also a "nation of immigrants." The number of Mexican Canadians remained small into the 1980s. Starting in the 1990s, many middle-class Mexicans began to immigrate to Canada: doctors, engineers, business owners, and others. Thousands of poor Mexicans came as legal temporary migrant laborers, especially to Ontario's fruit and vegetable fields and winter greenhouses.

From 1998 to 2003, the number of legal temporary Mexican workers in Canada rose by nearly 70 percent, from 13,300 to 22,300. Thousands get into the country just by showing their passports, and many stay and work illegally. With the Canadian government's official policy of encouraging immigration (unlike the United States) and promoting a multicultural society, it is likely that the number of Mexican Canadians will continue to rise rapidly. Today, Mexican-Canadian communities in big cities like Montreal, Toronto, Hamilton, Winnipeg, Calgary, and Vancouver are growing fast.[29]

MEXICAN-AMERICAN DEMOGRAPHICS

In order to understand where the United States is going, you need to know where it has been and where it is today. You have already learned a good deal about the Mexican-American past. What about the present? The following figures (drawn from the 2000 U.S. census unless stated otherwise) provide a snapshot of Mexican Americans compared to other Latinos and the rest of the U.S. population.[30] They also give a good idea of the kinds of questions demographers ask.

Spatial Distribution
- In 2000, Mexican Americans were concentrated in five Western states, with 55 percent living in California, Texas, Arizona, Nevada, and Colorado. The South was home to 32 percent; the Midwest, 11 percent; and the Northeast, 2 percent.

- In all of the 10 biggest cities in the United States—except New York—Mexican Americans were the largest Latino group. In New York, Puerto Ricans were the largest. Los Angeles had the biggest concentration of Latinos, with Mexican

Naturalized U.S. citizens are sworn in during the fifteenth annual Fiesta of Independence at South Mountain Community College, in Phoenix, Arizona, in 2003. Among the 280 new U.S. citizens were more than 90 Mexicans.

Americans making up about two-thirds of the total (1.1 million Mexican Americans in a Latino population of 1.7 million and a total population of 3.7 million).

Growth Patterns

- Mexican Americans are the fastest-growing ethnic group in the United States and have been for the past quarter century.

- From 1990 to 2000, the number of people in the United States who were born in Mexico more than doubled, from 4.3 million to 9.2 million—an increase of 114 percent.

- The five states with the biggest percent increases in their Mexican immigrant populations from 1990 to 2000 were

The 10 Largest Cities in the United States, with Latino and Mexican-American Population, 2000

City	Population			Latino Population		Mexican-Origin Population		
	Total	Rank	Latino	Rank	% of Total	Number	% of Total Latinos	% of Total Pop.
New York, NY	8,008,278	1	2,160,554	1	27.0	182,872	8.5	2.3
Los Angeles, CA	3,694,820	2	1,719,073	2	46.5	1,091,611	63.5	29.5
Chicago, IL	2,896,016	3	753,644	3	26.0	530,565	70.4	18.3
Houston, TX	1,953,631	4	730,865	4	37.4	527,684	72.2	27.0
Philadelphia, PA	1,517,550	5	128,928	24	8.5	6,220	4.8	0.4
Phoenix, AZ	1,321,045	6	449,972	6	34.1	375,277	83.4	28.4
San Diego, CA	1,223,400	7	310,752	9	25.4	259,167	83.4	21.2
Dallas, TX	1,188,580	8	422,587	8	35.6	350,325	82.9	29.5
San Antonio, TX	1,144,646	9	671,394	5	58.7	473,333	70.5	41.4
Detroit, MI	951,270	10	47,167	72	5.0	33,143	70.3	3.5

Source: U.S. Census Bureau. Available online at *http://www.census.gov/*

all in the South: Tennessee (2,166 percent), Alabama (2,054 percent), North Carolina (1,865 percent), Kentucky (1,637 percent), and South Carolina (1,377 percent). These are phenomenally high increases! These and other data show that Mexican-American communities are mushrooming in places where none had existed before.

• From 1990 to 2000, the growth in the Mexican-American population was split about evenly between immigration (53 percent of the growth) and "natural increase" among those already in the country (the difference between births and deaths; 47 percent).

Nativity and Citizenship

• Mexican Americans were the largest foreign-born authorized immigrant group in the United States—more than one-quarter of the nation's total (9 million out of 33 million foreign born).

• There were about 5 million undocumented Mexican immigrants, the most of any group.

• About 4 in 10 Mexican Americans were foreign born (42 percent), compared to about 1 in 10 for the general population (11 percent).

• Of people born in Mexico living in the United States, about two-thirds were citizens (68 percent). In the general population, 93 percent were citizens.

• The Mexican population as a whole has arrived very recently. Imagine that 100 people gathered in a room represent all Mexican Americans in the United States in 2000. When did these 100 people enter the room (the country)? Forty-five came between 1990 and 2000. Twenty-eight came in the decade before that (1980–1989), and 15 in the decade before that (1970–1979). Only eight were already in the room before 1970.

States with the Highest Population of Mexican Americans, 2000	
State	**Mexican-American Population**
California	8,455,926
Texas	5,071,963
Illinois	1,144,390
Arizona	1,065,578
Colorado	450,760

Language and Housing

- In 2000, four-fifths of Mexican Americans spoke a language other than English at home (79 percent), compared to one-fifth of the general population (18 percent).

- About half rented their homes (52 percent), and about half owned (48 percent). In the general population, about one-third rented (34 percent) and two-thirds owned (66 percent).

Age, Marital Status, and Fertility Rates

- Mexican Americans tended to be much younger than the general population, with a median age of 24.4, compared to 35.4 for the total population. More than one-third (37 percent) were younger than 18, compared to about one-quarter (26 percent) in the general population.

- More than one-third were never married (35 percent), compared to about one-quarter in the general population (27 percent). This was probably because of the high percentage of young unmarried Mexican-born men (and, increasingly, women) working on "the other side."

- More than four in five (84 percent) lived with other family members, compared to about two-thirds (68 percent) of the general population.

• Mexican-American women were having more babies than the general population of women (they had a higher fertility rate). On average, a woman of Mexican ancestry gave birth to 2.9 babies during her childbearing years, compared to an average of 1.8 babies for non-Hispanic women.

Poverty, Income, and Employment

• About one-quarter of people of Mexican descent lived in poverty (24 percent), twice as high a rate as the general population (12 percent).

• They earned a lot less on average, about 66 cents for every dollar earned by the general population; their median family income was $33,500, versus $50,000 for everyone else. For a year's work, Mexican-American women earned about three-

Among Mexican Americans, approximately 24 percent live in poverty, which is twice the rate of the national average. The Macias family, who immigrated to the United States from Guadalajara, Mexico, is pictured here outside their trailer in Colonia Pueblo de Palmas, Texas.

quarters as much as the general population of women; that is, their median yearly incomes were $20,600 and $27,200, respectively. Mexican-American men earned 64 cents for every dollar earned by men in the general population; that is, their median yearly incomes were $23,500 versus $37,000.

• Latinos were concentrated in lower-paying jobs, with two-thirds (67 percent) of the men working in service, construction, manufacturing, and transport, and three-quarters (75 percent) of the women working in service, sales and office, manufacturing, and transport.

• Unemployment was and is much higher—8.4 percent among Mexican Americans in 2002, compared to 5.1 percent for the general population.

Education

• Mexican Americans had lower educational levels than the general population, with more than half (54 percent) lacking a high school diploma, compared to one-fifth (20 percent) of the general population.

• Fewer than 1 in 12 had a bachelor's degree from college (8 percent). In the general population, about one in four (24 percent) did.

SUMMARY

In very broad strokes, these and other data paint a clear portrait of the situation of Mexican Americans today. On the whole, they are younger, poorer, more vulnerable to economic hard times, less educated, and more family oriented than the general population. Most strikingly, their communities are growing rapidly in almost every part of the country. Traditional hubs of Mexican immigration, such as San Diego, Los Angeles, Houston, Denver, and Chicago, continue to see rapidly climbing populations. Meanwhile, the growth rates in many nontraditional destinations that 20 years ago had virtually no Mexican-American residents is truly astounding—from medium-sized cities like Charlottesville, Virginia, to little towns like Norwalk, Wisconsin. As you read these words, Mexican Americans are reshaping the demographic map of North America in some very basic ways.

In what kinds of ways? The answer depends on many things. It depends on their relationships to dominant white culture and to other minority groups. It depends especially on how Mexican Americans see themselves—on how they understand who they are, as both Mexicans and Americans. The basic question all people ask themselves—"who am I?"—echoes loudly among Mexican Americans today. To understand their search for self-identity today and in the future, it helps to look into the past, to see how previous generations have wrestled with this same question.

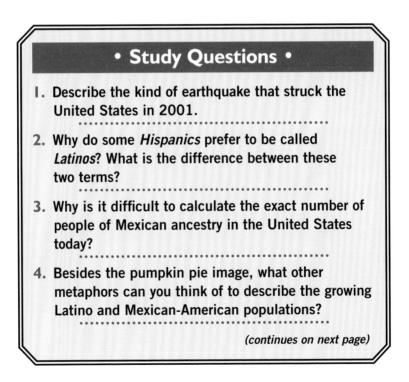

• Study Questions •

1. Describe the kind of earthquake that struck the United States in 2001.

2. Why do some *Hispanics* prefer to be called *Latinos*? What is the difference between these two terms?

3. Why is it difficult to calculate the exact number of people of Mexican ancestry in the United States today?

4. Besides the pumpkin pie image, what other metaphors can you think of to describe the growing Latino and Mexican-American populations?

(continues on next page)

(continued from previous page)

5. What metaphors have been used to describe the process by which immigrants become Americans? What are the strengths and weaknesses of these metaphors?

6. When describing the nation's growing Latino and Mexican populations, why should images of "floods" and "rising tides" be used with caution?

7. Can you think of any ethnic practices your family has kept from its country or countries of origin? Foods? Holidays? Music? Speech patterns? Ask the adults in your family if they remember anything about these "cultural retentions" from when they were growing up.

8. What is the most striking fact about Mexican immigration to the United States and Canada today, in your view?

6

Social Identity and Activism

QUESTIONS OF SOCIAL IDENTITY AND SOCIAL ACTION

About 2,500 years ago in ancient Greece, a very wise man named Socrates offered two words of advice: "Know thyself."

What does it mean, to "know thyself"? In part, it means knowing about the special qualities that make you unique. "My name is _____, and I am good at sports," you might say. Or, "I am very musical," or, "I like math." Those are aspects of your *personal* identity. There is more to your identity than just the personal, though. There is also your social identity. To know your social identity means knowing about your *social* relationships, about how you fit into the wider world: your friends, your family, your community, your nation. "I am friends with _____." "I belong to the _____ family." "I am a member of the _____ community." "My nationality is _____" (fill in the blanks).

Knowing your social identity is not always simple or easy, especially when you are a member of a minority group. In different times and places, people of Mexican ancestry in the United States have called themselves "Mexicans," "Mexican Americans," "Spaniards," "Spanish Americans," "Latin Americans," "*hispanos*," "*tejanos*," "*californios*," "Chicanos," "*Xicanos*," "*la raza*" ("the race" or "the people"), "Hispanics," "Latinos," and other names. Others have called them insulting names like "*pochos*," "wetbacks," "spics," and "*greasers*."

For Mexican Americans, creating a social identity very often has meant confronting the superior power of Anglos. The result has been a long series of struggles by many individuals and organizations, with the goals of making a better life and securing the rights of citizenship ("civil rights") as defined in the constitution and all the laws of the land. This chapter examines two examples of these struggles.

BARRIO BOY: THE STORY OF ERNESTO GALARZA

Stanford University, California, 1928. Under a blue sky and blazing sun, a young man with shining black hair, piercing brown eyes, and an armful of books walks briskly to his next class. He is a 23-year-old graduate student named Ernesto Galarza. Galarza is angry. He is angry when he thinks about all the injustices suffered every day by Mexican Americans like himself. His mind races with images of Mexican-American farm laborers toiling in the hot sun for pennies per day, the Anglo growers and bosses treating them like animals. His anger boils when he recalls prominent Anglos saying that Mexican immigration should be restricted because Mexicans are nothing more than "hordes of hungry dogs, filthy children with faces plastered with flies . . . human filth . . . stealing anything they can get their hands on . . . a menace to public health . . . a degenerate race."[31] He knows he has good reason for his anger, and he feels a responsibility to do something about it.

Ernesto Galarza had come to California from a small town in Mexico with his mother and two uncles when he was eight years old, fleeing the violence of the Mexican Revolution. When they arrived in California, they worked as migrant farm laborers. Like Rita and César Chávez a few years later, Ernesto learned from bitter experience about the injustices suffered by migrant workers. Because he was very smart and hard working, he was granted a scholarship to college and earned his undergraduate degree. He did so well that he became the first Mexican American admitted to Stanford University, where he earned a master's degree. After Stanford, he went to Columbia University in New York City, where he earned a Ph.D.

Ernesto Galarza went on to become one of the most remarkable and important Mexican Americans in the history of the United States. A writer, scholar, educator, activist, and organizer, he was nominated for the Nobel Peace Prize several times (he never won). His life's work was tied together by a single goal, which he pursued with dogged determination: to help improve the lives of working-class Latinos.

In 1948, after finishing his Ph.D., Galarza returned to California's fruit and vegetable fields to try to organize the migrant farmworkers for the American Federation of Labor, one of the nation's biggest unions. Chapter 1 mentions that, before César Chávez, many people had tried to organize the farmworkers and all had failed. Ernesto Galarza was one of those who tried. He failed mainly because of the Bracero Program, because the hundreds of thousands of braceros made it easy for California's growers to hire "replacement workers."

In 1950, for example, Galarza led a strike of thousands of tomato pickers in California's San Joaquin Valley who demanded above-poverty wages. In response, the growers brought in thousands of braceros to replace them. A year later, Galarza led a strike of cantaloupe pickers and, after that, of sugarcane workers and strawberry pickers in Louisiana. All of these strikes failed, and Galarza could clearly see why—because there were so many braceros. (Failures in life can sometimes be very valuable—*if* one learns from them.)

As a result of these failures, Galarza stopped trying to organize workers and devoted all of his efforts to abolishing the Bracero Program. "There was no choice," he said. "Without a frontal attack on the bracero program, nothing was possible. Farmworkers couldn't be organized, they couldn't have a union, they couldn't have any rights, as long as the program existed."[32]

For the next dozen years, Galarza worked to abolish the Bracero Program. He testified many times before Congress and government committees; gave speeches to school, church, and community groups; and issued hundreds of reports. He spent years among the braceros, talking to them, listening to their stories, and documenting the abuses they suffered. His first book, *Merchants of Labor: The Mexican Bracero Story* (1964), is considered a classic, "an outstanding account" that helped convince Congress to abolish the program.[33] In many ways, Galarza's work paved the way for César Chávez and the United Farm Workers of America.

Until his death in 1984 at age 78, Galarza continued his life's work of helping to improve the lives of working-class Latinos. He wrote many other books, including *Spiders in the House and Workers in the Field* (1970) and *Barrio Boy* (1971). The latter, a memoir of his boyhood journey from a small Mexican village to the hustle and bustle of California's capital city, is a marvelous read, perfect for middle-school students just like you.[34]

Throughout his life, Galarza remained proud of his Mexican ancestry. In the introduction to *Barrio Boy*, Galarza reflected on the issues of social identity that were swirling around in the 1960s and 1970s. Some people, he wrote, have spread the rumor that these Mexican immigrants and their offspring have lost their "self-image." By this, of course, they mean that a Mexican doesn't know what he is; and if by chance he is something, it isn't any good. I, for one Mexican, never had any doubts on this score. I can't remember a time when I didn't know who I was.[35]

Ernesto Galarza's life work provides ample testimony for his plainspoken and proud assertion of his social identity as both a Mexican and an American—but his was not the only approach.

LULAC: THE LEAGUE OF UNITED LATIN AMERICAN CITIZENS

Corpus Cristi, Texas, May 1929. With a drenching rain falling outside, delegates from three Mexican-American organizations meet for the first General Convention of the League of United Latin American Citizens (*LULAC*). LULAC is made up mainly of middle- and upper-class educated Mexican Americans who feel a need for a larger group to defend and protect their rights as citizens. Afraid of being called "Communists" or "anti-American," the group adopts the American flag as its flag, "America the Beautiful" as its song, and the "George Washington Prayer" as its prayer. Over the next few years, the organization grows rapidly in the Southwest and beyond, although it remains strongest in Texas.

LULAC believed in assimilation into the dominant Anglo culture. Its members were expected to speak English and be well groomed, neatly dressed, and polite, even in the face of anti-Mexican racism. LULAC generally did not challenge racism head-on. Rather, it tended to seek exceptions for its members, the "better class" of Mexican Americans. It worked mainly to desegregate public places like swimming pools, barber shops, restaurants, and parks, while generally ignoring the problems of working-class Mexican Americans. In the 1930s, for example,

The League of United Latin American Citizens (LULAC) first met in Corpus Cristi, Texas, in May 1929. LULAC's mission is to advance the economic condition, educational attainment, political influence, and health and civil rights of the Hispanic population.

LULAC supported the government's repatriation campaigns (see Chapter 2). It also opposed strikes by working-class Mexican Americans, like one by San Antonio's pecan shellers.

One of the most revealing things about LULAC is its name: League of United *Latin American* Citizens. By calling themselves "Latin Americans," LULAC's members downplayed their Mexican ancestry. Given Anglos' racist portrayals of Mexicans as poor, dirty, and disloyal, it is not hard to understand why. Rather than challenging those portrayals directly, LULAC tended to claim that its members were unlike poor "greasers" and so should be allowed to exercise their rights of citizenship.

This effort to obscure Mexican ancestry was common among middle- and upper-class people of Spanish descent in the areas conquered in the Mexican-American War. This was especially true among wealthy tejanos of Texas, hispanos of New Mexico, and californios of California, who often called themselves Spanish to distance themselves from poorer Mexican Americans. Sometimes it worked and they were able to pass as white, living and working alongside Anglos. More often, they found it impossible to escape Anglos' anti-Mexican feelings. To many Anglos, one greaser was the same as another.

Some working-class Mexican Americans thought that these so-called "Spanish Americans" were foolish to deny their Mexican identity. Writer Richard Rodriguez, for example, the son of working-class parents, remembered growing up in California in the 1950s and 1960s:

> "We are Mexicans," my mother and father would say, and taught their four children to say. . . . My mother and father scorned those "white" Mexican-Americans who tried to pass themselves off as Spanish. My parents would never have thought of denying their ancestry. I never denied it: My ancestry is Mexican.[36]

On the whole, LULAC represented the interests and identity of the "Spanish Americans" described here by Richard Rodriguez. It is also true that, for many years, LULAC was the only nationwide Mexican-American organization devoted to defending the civil rights of persons of Mexican ancestry. In the face of enormous hostility and racism, LULAC's leaders fought courageously to protect the dignity and rights of thousands of Mexican Americans.[37]

Women played a very important role in LULAC. Many cities and towns had a Ladies LULAC, where women met to discuss and act on the issues of the day. Some Ladies LULAC members, such as Alice Dickerson Montemayor, challenged traditional gender roles among Mexican Americans. A social worker and head of the Ladies LULAC in Laredo, Texas, Montemayor encouraged women to vote, become educated, and work outside the home. Her husband was not a member of LULAC. "Men's LULAC had nothing to do with us,"[38] she recalled. Ladies LULAC activists like Montemayor helped pave the way for later generations of Mexican-American women activists, a topic explored in the next chapter.

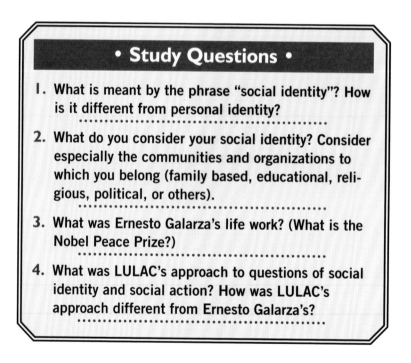

• Study Questions •

1. What is meant by the phrase "social identity"? How is it different from personal identity?

2. What do you consider your social identity? Consider especially the communities and organizations to which you belong (family based, educational, religious, political, or others).

3. What was Ernesto Galarza's life work? (What is the Nobel Peace Prize?)

4. What was LULAC's approach to questions of social identity and social action? How was LULAC's approach different from Ernesto Galarza's?

7

The Chicano Years

In 1951, Oliver Brown, an African-American man in Topeka, Kansas, sued the local school board because they refused to let his eight-year-old daughter, Linda, attend a nearby school. That school, said the school board, was for white children. Instead, every day, Linda had to walk past that school on her way to a bus stop, where she was picked up and taken to a school for black children. Oliver Brown did not think that was fair or in keeping with the promise of America as a land of equality and freedom. The local federal court ruled against his lawsuit, but Brown was determined. He appealed, and three years later, the case reached the U.S. Supreme Court. In a unanimous and earth-shattering decision, the Supreme Court ruled in *Brown v. Board of Education* (1954) that racial segregation in public schools was unconstitutional. The ruling overturned nearly 60 years of legal precedent. Ever since the *Plessy v. Ferguson* case of

1896, racial segregation in public facilities had been legal. Now, after 1954, it was not.

The 1950s, 1960s, and 1970s saw huge changes in American society. African Americans, women, Latinos, Native American Indians, and other groups became increasingly insistent in demanding their freedoms and rights. Sometimes they formed partnerships or coalitions with other groups to strengthen their efforts. These years saw a flowering of struggles by people of Mexican ancestry to exercise their rights, to build coalitions, and to create a shared social identity. We have already explored some of these struggles, especially those of César Chávez and the farmworkers' movement.

This chapter examines four other leaders and groups of the 1960s and 1970s: (1) Reies López Tijerina and the Federal Alliance of Land Grants; (2) Rodolfo "Corky" Gonzales and the *Crusade for Justice*; (3) José Angel Gutiérrez and *La Raza Unida* (The United Race, or People's) Party; and (4) Vilma Martínez and the Mexican-American Legal Defense and Educational Fund (*MALDEF*). Understanding the actions and beliefs of these leaders and organizations will, it is hoped, enrich your understanding of the complexity and diversity of the Mexican-American experience.

REIES LÓPEZ TIJERINA AND THE FEDERAL ALLIANCE OF LAND GRANTS

Tierra Amarilla, New Mexico, June 5, 1967. As the sun beats down on the surrounding pine-covered mountains, 20 Mexican-American men armed with hunting rifles and a piece of paper called an arrest warrant suddenly arrive at the courthouse in the small town of Tierra Amarilla in northern New Mexico. They are members of the Federal Alliance of Land Grants (*Alianza Federal de Pueblos Libres*, or "Alianza"), and they are making a raid on the courthouse. They plan to make a citizen's arrest of the local district attorney.

A district attorney is a county prosecutor, the government official whose job is to convict criminals and send them to jail. A citizen's arrest occurs when ordinary citizens arrest someone for breaking the law. By the Alianza's reasoning, the district attorney had broken the law (you will see how in a minute), so what they are doing is entirely legal. They are raiding the courthouse to arrest the government official whose job it is to arrest people!

On this hot afternoon, the district attorney is not in the courthouse. In the scuffle and confusion, Alianza members accidentally wound two police officers. They flee into the hills, taking another police officer and a reporter with them. The police chase them with hunting dogs, armed men on horseback, cars, and helicopters. The Alianza's leader is later arrested and charged with attempted murder and kidnapping. The events in Tierra Amarilla make headlines around the world.

To understand these events, you need to know something about the history of the Southwest (which by now you do) and the goals of the Alianza's leader. Reies López Tijerina was born in San Antonio, Texas, in 1923, the son of migrant farm laborers. In his youth, he became painfully aware of his and other Mexican Americans' poverty, lack of opportunity, and especially lack of land. When he was 17, he entered a Bible school, where he learned to read and write. He became a preacher and traveled throughout Mexico and the Southwest.[39]

After a while, Tijerina moved to northern New Mexico, where he learned about local struggles to recover lost lands— what was known as the "land-grant" issue. Many local Mexican Americans (hispanos), whose families had lived in that area for generations, believed that the big landowners in New Mexico, including the state and federal governments, had cheated them out of their rights to the land guaranteed in the Treaty of Guadalupe Hidalgo in 1848. For several years, Tijerina spent all of his spare time digging through old records and papers

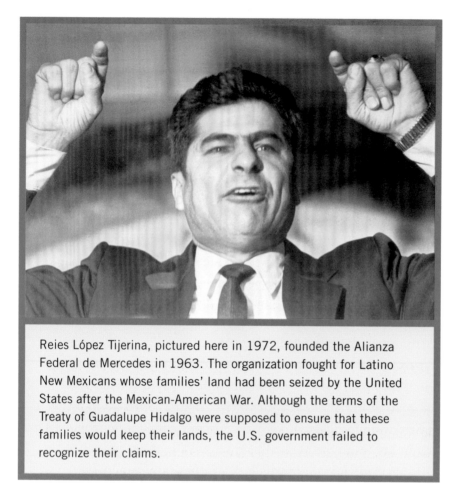

Reies López Tijerina, pictured here in 1972, founded the Alianza Federal de Mercedes in 1963. The organization fought for Latino New Mexicans whose families' land had been seized by the United States after the Mexican-American War. Although the terms of the Treaty of Guadalupe Hidalgo were supposed to ensure that these families would keep their lands, the U.S. government failed to recognize their claims.

in libraries and archives in New Mexico, Mexico, Spain, and Washington, D.C. The more he learned, the more he became convinced that Mexican-American villagers were the land's legal owners. In 1963, he formed the Alianza to get back the lands that he claimed were stolen more than 100 years before. He faced a huge challenge, because his adversary was the government itself.

Tijerina and the Alianza did everything they could to make their case heard. First, they tried to get the courts to recognize hispanos' land rights. Time and again they failed, so they tried something more dramatic. In 1966, they marched from Albuquerque to the state capital in Santa Fe to meet with the governor (he left just before they arrived). Later, they tried to take over part of Carson National Forest, which Tijerina claimed was part of a land grant stolen by the federal government years before. They even "arrested" two U.S. forest rangers for trespassing.

All of this was taking place while César Chávez and the UFWA were striking against the grape growers in California. By this time, the Alianza had more than 20,000 members. Then, the following June, came the events in Tierra Amarilla.

Reies López Tijerina was sent to prison for more than two years for his role in the Tierra Amarilla episode. He later ran for governor (he lost) and tried to arrest Supreme Court nominee Warren Burger (he failed). In the end, the Alianza reclaimed no lands.

Do all these failures mean that the Alianza movement was a failure? In its immediate aim, yes. It succeeded as well, however, bringing a great deal of attention to issues of Mexican Americans' rights and identity. Partly because of Tijerina and the Alianza, newspapers, magazines, radio programs, and TV shows began to pay closer attention to issues of social justice and civil rights among Mexican Americans across the country.

Among the Alianza's supporters were César Chávez, Martin Luther King, Jr., and other civil rights leaders. One very enthusiastic supporter was named Rodolfo "Corky" Gonzalez.

RODOLFO "CORKY" GONZALES AND THE CRUSADE FOR JUSTICE

Denver, Colorado, March 1969. In a huge auditorium near downtown, 1,500 young Mexican Americans gather for the first annual Chicano Youth Liberation Conference. It is a noisy, colorful, energetic affair, more like a celebration than a conference. Among the participants are professors, farmworkers, gang members, and ex-convicts. Mostly, the auditorium is filled with students from high schools and colleges across the country, young people coming together to define, celebrate, and act on their new social identity as Chicanos.

A few years before, in the mid-1960s, many young Mexican Americans in California, Colorado, and elsewhere began to call themselves *Chicanos* to describe their new identity. This term, derived from "Mexicano," long had been used by Anglos as an insult to Mexican Americans. Now, in the mid-1960s, young Mexican Americans took this word, filled it with new meaning, and applied it to themselves. As they saw it, "Mexican American" failed to describe who they really were. They were Mexican and they were American, but they were more. They were Chicanos.

The organizer of the Denver conference was a 41-year-old activist named Rodolfo "Corky" Gonzales. Born and raised in Denver's tough eastside Mexican *barrio*, Gonzales represented the "new breed" of Mexican American: urban, militant, outspoken, committed to making social change happen. Like Ernesto Galarza and thousands of others, Corky's parents had migrated to the United States as youngsters, fleeing the violence of the Mexican Revolution. Corky's mother died when he was only two years old, leaving his father to raise the family's eight children. Telling many stories about his life in Mexico, Corky's father instilled in his children a fierce pride in their heritage.

Very smart and valuing education but unable to afford college, Corky became a champion boxer. After retiring from prize fighting, he opened a small business and became active in the local Democratic Party. He soon became fed up with the slow pace of change. In 1965, inspired by the African-American civil rights movement, Corky resigned from the Democratic Party and founded a civil rights and cultural organization called the Crusade for Justice. It was the nation's first organization devoted to defense of the civil rights of all Mexican Americans.

Unlike the United Farm Workers in California and the Alianza in New Mexico, the Crusade for Justice was based in the city, not the countryside. Unlike LULAC, its members were mostly young and working class. Its goals went beyond issues of land and civil rights to include redefining what it meant to be Mexican American.

In 1967, Corky Gonzales wrote a poem that had a huge influence on the Chicano movement. Called "I am Joaquín," the poem wrestled with issues of social identity at the core of this emerging movement. The poem was discussed widely at the 1969 conference. Many found it deeply moving. It helped inspire conference participants to write an important new document, *El Plan Espirtual de Aztlán* (the "Spiritual Plan of Aztlán").

The conference participants believed that every nation, every group of people with a shared social identity, needs a homeland. African Americans could look to Africa, Asian Americans to Asia, Native Americans to the Americas. According to the *Plan Espiritual,* Chicanos' homeland was a place called *Aztlán,* somewhere in the Southwest. No one knew exactly where Aztlán was, but that did not mean that it was not real, at least in people's imaginations. The shared belief in this mythical homeland was meant to help Chicanos rediscover their social identity, especially their Native American Indian heritage.

Corky Gonzales and his Chicano "brothers and sisters" at the youth conference promoted what is called "cultural nationalism." They believed that all Chicanos formed a kind of nation, with a shared history, culture, and heritage. Their goal was to rediscover this heritage. Not everyone agreed with this cultural nationalism, however: Some critics argued that, by stressing their shared culture and heritage, they neglected issues of poverty, unemployment, and class divisions.

Another important criticism came from female Chicanos, or *Chicanas,* who criticized the conference for its all-male leadership. Many were angry that the movement and its male leaders ignored issues important to women—especially unequal sharing of housework, child care, sexism, and gender stereotypes, such as the idea that women are better at cleaning than men or that men make better leaders than women. Feminist Chicanas, or *Xicanas*, insisted that the struggle for equality *among* Chicanos was necessary for the freedom and equality of *all* Chicanos. (Sometimes "Chicano" was spelled "Xicano"; the "X" comes from the ancient language of the Aztecs and is pronounced like "ch.")

One of the most important things to come out of the 1969 conference was a call to create a new political party—neither Democrat nor Republican—to represent all Chicanos. A few months later, a young activist in Texas named José Angel Gutiérrez rose to the challenge.

JOSÉ ANGEL GUTIÉRREZ AND *EL PARTIDO RAZA UNIDA*

Crystal City, Texas, January 17, 1970. Along the asphalt highway leading into Crystal City, Texas, after passing miles and miles of flat green fields, a big sign reads, "Welcome to Crystal City, Spinach Capital of the World." On this midwinter day in 1970, 300 Mexican Americans are packed into a meeting hall near downtown. After much discussion, the meeting ends on a very hopeful note. The participants have formed a new political party. They call it *El Partido Raza Unida* ("The United People's Party").

The meeting's main organizer is 25-year-old activist José Angel Gutiérrez. Son of a Mexican-born physician, Gutiérrez was born and raised in Crystal City. He went to college in San Antonio, where he and some other students founded the Mexican American Youth Organization (MAYO). One of MAYO's main goals was to get high schools and colleges to pay more attention to Mexican and Mexican-American history and culture. They also believed that high schools and colleges should do more to help Spanish-speaking students, who were disadvantaged because of their poor command of English. *Bilingual education*, they believed, was the answer. Bilingual education involves teaching students mainly in their native tongue until they have mastered their adopted language. MAYO also believed that Mexican-American workers should be paid higher wages and have better working conditions.

The best way to achieve these goals, they thought, was to get Mexican Americans elected to local political offices. A few months after the meeting in Crystal City, La Raza Unida won seats on the city council and school board in Crystal City and neighboring towns. Soon after, La Raza Unida parties were organized in California and Colorado. Corky Gonzales organized the one in Colorado. Hopes were running high.

In 1972, La Raza Unida held a national convention in El Paso, Texas. Here, La Raza Unida showed that it was far from unified. Corky Gonzales headed the Colorado branch of the party, José Angel Gutiérrez the Texas branch. They had very different ideas about the party's goals. Corky believed that the party should work mainly on building Chicanos' social identity and sense of cultural nationalism. José Angel wanted to focus more on winning local and state elections. The divisions between these two leaders and their backers weakened La Raza Unida. The party broke up into factions, and many of its members abandoned it. By the mid-1970s, the party was no longer an important political force, in Texas, Colorado, or anywhere else. A few years later, La Raza Unida had essentially disbanded.[40]

Although some Chicano organizations of these years were like shooting stars, shining brightly before fizzling out, others were less visible but had a huge impact long after they were formed. An excellent example is Vilma Martínez and an organization called MALDEF.

VILMA MARTÍNEZ AND THE MEXICAN AMERICAN LEGAL DEFENSE AND EDUCATIONAL FUND (MALDEF)

San Antonio, Texas, 1960. Sitting across from the paper-cluttered desk of her high school counselor, a young, bright-eyed

Mexican-American woman describes her goal of going to college and becoming a lawyer. Her fresh-faced excitement turns to anger when the counselor replies that such ambitious goals are just not realistic for a girl like her. It might seem like a good idea, he explains, but really it would be a big waste of time and money because she will just end up marrying, having children, and staying at home.

The young woman, Vilma Martínez, is disappointed but not discouraged. Her self-confidence, rooted in her grandmother's lessons and love, gives her the inner knowledge that she can do anything she puts her mind to. Born in 1943 in San Antonio, Texas, the eldest of her Texan mother and Mexican father's five children, Vilma spent much of her girlhood cleaning house and caring for her siblings. At age 15, she worked in a lawyer's office in San Antonio. She really liked it. The work was very interesting and challenging. Ignoring her counselor, she applied to the University of Texas, where she earned her diploma in only two and a half years.

Soon after, in 1967, she graduated from Columbia Law School in New York City, one of only 20 women in a class of 300 students. She was especially interested in civil rights. Laws that discriminated against women and minorities had no place in American life, she thought, and she was determined to change them. First, she worked for the National Association for the Advancement of Colored People (NAACP), one of the country's leading civil rights organizations. Soon after, she helped found an organization devoted to Mexican-American civil rights, the Mexican American Legal Defense and Educational Fund (MALDEF).

In 1973, at age 29, Martínez became MALDEF's president. For the next 10 years, she led this increasingly important organization, challenging discriminatory laws and winning many civil rights legal battles. MALDEF also fought hard for bilingual education and public schooling for undocumented immigrants. In 1982, it won a very important case before the U.S. Supreme Court that guaranteed all children the right to public education, regardless of their citizenship. Vilma and MALDEF also helped create laws to make ballots in both English and Spanish so that citizens who did not read English could still exercise their constitutional right to vote.

Vilma went on to hold many other important positions, including chair of the governing board of the University of California. President Jimmy Carter asked her to sit on the committee that chose ambassadors to foreign countries. He also named her to lead a group that would make sure that Mexican Americans were properly counted in the 1980 U.S. census. Because of this group's work, Mexican Americans gained much more political power than they had had before.

From the 1980s to the present, Vilma Martínez has earned many awards and honors for her civil rights work. Not as well known as other Chicano leaders, she has made, and continues to make, a tremendous difference in the lives of millions of Mexican Americans.[41]

LEGACIES OF THE CHICANO YEARS

By the 1980s, the energy and enthusiasm of the "Chicano generation" had faded. Younger generations of Mexican Americans tended to focus more on getting good educations and building careers and showed less interest in Chicano politics or cultural nationalism. Still, the changes of the 1960s left a huge and lasting legacy. The insistence that Mexican Americans enjoy the full rights of citizenship, backed by the civil rights laws of the 1950s and 1960s, meant that they no longer had to see or obey signs that read "No Mexicans or Dogs" or stay silent in the face of discrimination. By the mid-1970s, with the illimination of Jim Crow laws—their supporters put up quite a fight before the laws actually died—it was no longer legal to discriminate in public against anyone, anywhere, because of skin color or national origin.

These years also saw the creation of many other organizations
that had a huge impact through the 1980s and after. For example,
thanks mainly to MEChA (*Movimiento Estudiantíl Chicano de
Aztlán*, or Student Movement of Chicanos of Aztlán), Chicano
and Mexican-American Studies programs were created at
many colleges and universities across the country. Many are
thriving today. Another organization, the National Council of
La Raza (NCLR), became very active and influential. Its parent
organization was created in 1968, largely through the efforts of

By the 1960s and '70s, Chicano activism ensured that many
Mexican Americans were no longer discriminated against in public
places. Signs such as this one, which were used to keep Mexican
Americans out of restaurants, were no longer commonplace.

none other than Ernesto Galarza. Today, the NCLR is one of the nation's leading organizations, advocating for Latinos in crucial areas of public policy, from housing and health care to education and immigration reform.

The Chicano activism of the 1960s and 1970s also forced many Anglos to confront their racism and bigotry. Many, especially the younger generations, learned to respect Mexican Americans as fellow human beings and fellow Americans. Despite its weaknesses, the Chicano movement changed the country in lasting ways. Along with the other social movements of these years—of African Americans, women, Native American Indians, opponents of the Vietnam War, and others—the Chicano movement helped create a more inclusive and tolerant America. Still, as events since the 1970s show, the United States has a long way to go before it achieves its ideals of political equality and equal opportunity for all.

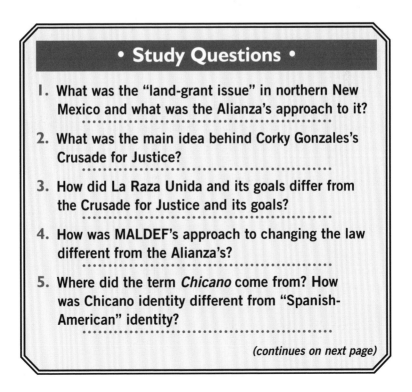

• Study Questions •

1. What was the "land-grant issue" in northern New Mexico and what was the Alianza's approach to it?

2. What was the main idea behind Corky Gonzales's Crusade for Justice?

3. How did La Raza Unida and its goals differ from the Crusade for Justice and its goals?

4. How was MALDEF's approach to changing the law different from the Alianza's?

5. Where did the term *Chicano* come from? How was Chicano identity different from "Spanish-American" identity?

(continues on next page)

(continued from previous page)

6. What were some of the legacies of the Chicano movement? What were its strengths and weaknesses?
   ....

7. Which of the individuals or groups in these two chapters do you find most admirable? Why?
   ....

8

Problems, Challenges, Debates, 1970s–2000s

For nearly three decades after World War II, the U.S. economy boomed. Average standards of living rose sharply, and there were plenty of good-paying jobs. That began to change in the mid-1970s, with the decline of manufacturing in the Northeast and Midwest and the rise of the "Sun Belt" in the South and Southwest. Industrial giants like General Motors moved more factories overseas, where labor was cheaper. Unemployment rose as jobs became lower-paying and oriented toward service industries like retail, fast food, and information processing. Rural America changed, too, with the rise of "agribusiness" and the decline of family farms.

On the Mexican side of the border, many U.S. companies built huge factories, called *maquiladoras*, where Mexican workers, mainly young women, assembled items such as clothing and electronic goods for sale in the United States. The main reason for the rise of maquiladoras was that Mexican labor was cheaper than American workers. In the rest of Mexico, the economy barely kept pace with rising population. Meanwhile, radio, newspapers, and television brought images of U.S. wealth and affluence to millions of Mexican homes and families. Also, many Mexicans had relatives already in the United States. All of these pressures drove millions of Mexicans to seek a better life on "the other side."

THE UNDOCUMENTED

What are the main problems and challenges that Mexican immigrants face today? Here again you need to understand the huge differences between authorized and unauthorized immigrants. Legal immigrants enjoy all the rights of citizenship and can use the law and the courts to defend their rights. For illegal immigrants, things are much harder. Fears of la migra, of deportation, and of being separated from their families mean that they have a much harder time defending their rights.

What are those rights? In fact, they are quite broad. In 1982, the U.S. Supreme Court ruled that no child can be denied public education because of his or her legal status (under Vilma Martínez, MALDEF had brought the case to the Supreme Court). Federal law also requires hospitals to provide emergency care to everyone regardless of whether he or she is a citizen. Many states and cities also have laws and customary procedures that guarantee certain rights to everyone.[42]

Still, many undocumented immigrants are not aware of their rights. Also, because it can jail them, deport them, and break up their families, the government can inflict great harm on undocumented immigrants. Predictably, immigrants tend to stay away from government agencies.

Consider what that means. Think about all the services the government provides and rights it guarantees: freedom of speech and assembly; freedom from unreasonable search and seizure; the right to vote; equal protection of the law; public K–12 schools, colleges, and universities; student loans; public

Many illegal immigrants are wary of using services provided by the U.S. government, such as hospital care. Pictured here is Alejandra Ruiz, a Mexican immigrant from Michoacan, with her two-month-old daughter, in a hospital emergency room in Salinas, California.

parks; public libraries; public transportation; public hospitals; public roads; drivers' licenses; the police; the courts; social security; Medicare and Medicaid. Think about what it would mean to avoid these public services and avoid exercising your basic civil rights in everyday life.

The question that faces U.S. citizens and their government is, "What is the best public policy toward unauthorized immigrants?" Is it better to tighten the borders and create conditions in which they fear and avoid the government and are excluded from public life? Or, is it better to integrate them into public life? These questions promise to remain a matter of fierce debate. As the *New York Times* editorialized in late 2005:

In bits and pieces, communities all over the country are trying desperately to deal with what is really an immense national problem. Only Washington can untangle an immigration mess that draws a growing number of illegal immigrants across the nation's borders every year. . . . It's time for Congress and the president to do their jobs.[43]

As you have seen, this "immense national problem" has deep social and economic causes rooted in Mexico's poverty and American wealth and opportunities. Because changes in U.S. policies and laws do not address these causes, they seem unlikely to solve the problem.

AMNESTY: THE 1986 IMMIGRATION REFORM AND CONTROL ACT

In the mid-1980s, the federal government faced a huge outcry to do something about illegal immigration. It responded by passing an important amnesty law called the Immigration Reform and Control Act (IRCA) of 1986. The law said that people who could prove that they had lived in the United States since 1982 could become temporary legal residents, the first step toward becoming legal permanent residents and, eventually, U.S. citizens. More than 2.7 million people received amnesty under the law, including nearly 2 million Mexicans. Today, most of these former "illegal aliens" are citizens.

The IRCA also called for additional staff to be added to the U.S. Border Patrol and stiffer penalties against employers who knew that they were hiring undocumented workers. The law's supporters hoped that it would reduce the number of illegal immigrants. For several years, it did. By the early 1990s, however, the number of illegal immigrants started to rise again. It is still climbing. As the authors of one careful study concluded, "IRCA does not appear to have discouraged illegal immigration in the long run."[44] Something as complex and deeply rooted as illegal immigration is unlikely to decline only through changes in U.S. laws. Meanwhile, through the 1990s, as record numbers of undocumented immigrants crossed the nation's borders, the debate about what to do about it intensified.

ENDING THE "ILLEGAL ALIEN INVASION"

A good example of that debate took place in California, where in 1994, voters passed Proposition 187. Called "Save Our State" by its supporters, the law required the state's public schools to expel the children of unauthorized immigrants. It also required the state of California and local governments to stop providing nonemergency publicly funded health care to undocumented migrants, including children and pregnant women.

Proposition 187 claimed that the people of California "have suffered and are suffering economic hardship caused by the presence of illegal aliens . . . have suffered and are suffering personal injury and damage caused by the criminal conduct of illegal aliens . . . [and] have a right to the protection of their government from any person or persons entering this country unlawfully."[45] Its backers argued that Proposition 187 would end the "illegal alien invasion"[46] because public education, publicly funded health care, and social welfare benefits were like magnets that drew illegal immigrants to California.

Its opponents argued that Proposition 187 was offensive, foolish, and dangerous. The law would make it much harder for millions of people in the nation's most populous state to integrate into society, they claimed, and would create a huge population of uneducated and unhealthy children.

Californians passed Proposition 187 by a 59 percent majority. It was never put into effect, however. Within days, the courts issued a temporary restraining order against it and a few years later ruled it unconstitutional. Still, Proposition 187 showed how far some people were willing to go to strip away the rights of undocumented immigrants. Support for the law was not

In 1994, the state of California passed Proposition 187, which was intended to deny illegal immigrants social services, health care, and public education. The law, however, never went into effect because it was ruled unconstitutional. Pictured here is David Cervantes, one of the organizers of the "anti Prop 187" campaign.

limited to Anglos and African Americans. In fact, a surprisingly large number of Latinos voted for it, too.

From the 1990s to the present, local efforts to restrict the rights of undocumented immigrants have cropped up around the country. A good example is Canyon County, Idaho. In the early 2000s, Mexican-American County Commissioner Robert Vasquez launched a drive to end what he called "an imminent invasion" from Mexico. According to Vasquez, "the newcomers overwhelm public services, bring gang violence and drugs, spread diseases like tuberculosis, and insist on rights that should not be granted to non-citizens." "If I were governor," Vasquez declared, "I would close the borders of Idaho and mobilize the National Guard to secure checkpoints against all illegal aliens."[47]

Some Canyon County residents supported his efforts, but others strongly opposed them. "What he's done is cause a lot of divisions within this community," said one community activist. "If you're brown, you're targeted. But the Latino community is united against him."[48] The debate in Canyon County continues, as it does across the country.

BORDER VIGILANTISM

The fight against "illegal aliens" can also be seen in the efforts of vigilante groups along the border (a vigilante is someone who takes the law into his or her own hands). An example is the Minuteman Project in southern Arizona. "You . . . look out the window and what do you see?" its leader asked. "Hordes of illegals running from the bushes."[49] The group's goal is to end illegal immigration by forcing the U.S. Border Patrol to enforce immigration laws.

Since the 1990s, many other vigilante groups, including Ranch Rescue, American Border Patrol, and Friends of the Border Patrol, have formed in California, Texas, and elsewhere. Such groups are held together by their shared dislike of nonwhite illegal immigrants. Ranch Rescue's founder once described

Latinos as "dog turds." Migrants tell many stories of abuse and violence at the hands of such "citizen volunteers."

In March 2003, Ranch Rescue members beat two Salvadorans trying to enter the country illegally. Months later, with the help of the Southern Poverty Law Center and MALDEF, the Salvadorans sued Ranch Rescue and the owner of the ranch where the group was headquartered. The Salvadorans won, the owner lost his ranch, one of Ranch Rescue's leaders was imprisoned, and Ranch Rescue basically fell apart.

This was a rare instance of border justice. In most cases, vigilante groups are not prosecuted for breaking the law. In late 2005, there were more than 40 vigilante groups in the borderlands and beyond, detaining and sometimes brutalizing undocumented migrants. Their efforts are often supported by racist hate groups.[50]

Under President George W. Bush, the federal government has tended to look favorably on these citizen volunteers. In mid-2005, the commissioner of United States Customs and Border Protection said his agency was looking into ways "of having citizens that would be willing to volunteer to help the Border Patrol . . . something akin to a Border Patrol auxiliary."[51] His comments provoked a firestorm of protest from civil rights organizations.

Other groups help illegal migrants as they undertake the dangerous journey through the desert. In 2002, in El Paso, Texas, Mexican-born U.S. citizen Armando Alarcón started an organization called Countrymen to the Rescue. He felt that he had to do something after the U.S. Border Patrol found the body of an eight-year-old girl in the desert. Alarcón bought an old Cessna airplane and began to parachute bottles of water to migrants. By 2005, the group had about a dozen volunteers. Theirs is a humanitarian organization whose goal is to save lives. Some criticize the group: As one of the Minutemen said, "If you don't want to die, don't come."[52]

Two California Minutemen patrol the U.S.–Mexico border near Campo, California. The Minutemen are one of more than 40 volunteer groups who often mete out their own form of justice by abusing immigrants who cross into the United States illegally.

HOUSING RESTRICTIONS, ID CARDS, DRIVERS' CERTIFICATES, AND MORE

The issue of illegal immigration is especially acute in suburbs, currently the destination of most immigrants. Housing is generally cheaper in suburbs, and that is where most jobs are. "Immigration has become a local issue because . . . there is no federal policy in place," said one expert. "Local officials don't want to be responsible, but they have to respond to local concerns."[53]

Some officials take a hard line, arguing that "illegal immigrants are taking over our community" and "eroding our quality of life."[54] Numerous towns have passed new housing codes that forbid anyone from sleeping in a room other than a bedroom (immigrant households tend to be crowded). Other towns have passed laws that limit street parking and the square footage of driveways (immigrant households tend to have a lot of adults and cars). Still others have tried to use local laws against trespassing to limit the number of undocumented residents.[55]

Other communities have welcomed new immigrants. Some have opened hiring halls for job seekers rather than having them cluster on street corners or outside building-supply stores. In 2005, Tennessee began to issue "driving certificates" to undocumented immigrants. These permit them to drive but, unlike driver's licenses, cannot be used as ID cards. In a sense, the effort here is to document the undocumented.[56]

Other states and cities are experimenting with similar measures. In late 2005, the mayor of New Haven, Connecticut, proposed that the city issue identification cards to unauthorized immigrants. The idea's supporters said that the cards would make it easier for illegal immigrants to integrate into city life. They could get library cards and open bank accounts and would be less likely to be robbed. Opponents disagreed. "If people in Mexico got word that New Haven was giving out ID cards, what's going to happen?" asked one resident. "More people are going to come."[57] The controversy in New Haven and elsewhere continues.

HOUSING DISCRIMINATION AND SCHOOL SEGREGATION

Closely related to housing restrictions is the issue of housing discrimination. Illegal since the Fair Housing Act of 1968 and later laws, discrimination in housing based on race, national origin, religion, gender, and disability is very hard to prove. Landlords have the right to decide whether they have a house or apartment to rent and to select their tenants based on other factors, such as a person's references or whether he or she has a steady job. An investigation by the *Los Angeles Times* in 2001 found that housing discrimination in Los Angeles was widespread, with housing managers tending to favor those of their own ethnic and racial background.

Many housing rights activists and groups agree. Frances Espinosa of the Housing Rights Center in Los Angeles, for instance, said that her agency had received nearly 1,400 complaints from June 2003 to June 2004. "We have seen many cases where recent immigrants, especially those from Mexico and elsewhere in Latin America, have been targeted because landlords think they won't complain,"[58] Espinosa said. The federal government earmarks only about $10 million per year for enforcing fair housing laws, most of which goes to cases of alleged discrimination against blacks, people with children, and the disabled. Overall, the evidence suggests that housing discrimination against Mexican Americans remains very common.

Housing discrimination is closely linked to school segregation, because most children attend public schools nearest to their homes. A 2005 study by Harvard University's Civil Rights Project found that, in practice, racial segregation in U.S. public schools actually had increased since the landmark *Brown v. Board of Education* decision 50 years earlier, especially in the South but in fact all over the country. The exploding Latino population in the South and elsewhere has meant not only continuing discrimination in housing and employment, but also increasingly segregated public schools, issues that are very tightly bound together.[59]

BILINGUAL EDUCATION

Learning English is one of the hardest tasks that faces Mexican immigrants. For Spanish speakers, English is very difficult. Overall, it is much easier for English speakers to learn Spanish than vice versa. This is because, in Spanish, words are pronounced exactly as written (*"se pronuncia como se escribe"*). English, on the other hand, has a zillion exceptions (as you surely know!), with its silent letters, odd spellings, and peculiar sounds. For speakers of other languages, English can be extremely difficult to learn.

One of the biggest debates since the 1970s has centered on the issue of bilingual education in public schools. In 1968, the Bilingual Education Act (backed by Supreme Court decisions and other laws) required public schools to offer equal opportunities to students with limited English skills. The result was the growth of bilingual education and English as a second language (ESL) programs in school districts across the country. Such programs had mixed results. A large body of research showed that bilingual education worked better than English immersion in helping kids learn English. Other studies showed that bilingual education was worse than English immersion. It was, and remains, a huge debate.

Meanwhile, groups that opposed bilingual education became increasingly active and powerful. English First and similar organizations argued that national unity requires a single language and that it should be English. In 1998, California voters passed Proposition 227, which severely restricted bilingual education programs. A similar law was passed in Arizona in 2000. Also, in 2002, the Republican Congress let the Bilingual Education Act of 1968 expire. Bilingual education is currently on the decline. In this area, too, the debate still swirls.

SUMMARY

This chapter has surveyed some of the key issues on Mexican immigration from the 1970s to the present, focusing on the problems and challenges that face unauthorized immigrants. What can be concluded from this survey? Perhaps most basically, you can say that these problems are very complex, that they have no easy answers, and that they promise to be with us for a long time to come. It also seems clear that ordinary people have an important role to play in responding to these challenges in ways that preserve America's promise as a land of political equality and equal opportunity for all.

VALUABLE RESOURCES THAT HELP REVEAL YOUR LINEAGE

Research is the art and science of asking and answering questions. The first step in any research project is to figure out the questions you would like to answer. Let's say you want to know about your family tree and how far back you can trace it. The best place to begin is to interview members of your own family: your parent(s), grandparent(s), aunts, uncles, and anyone else who knows about your family history. Begin in the present and work backward into the past. Ask who was born when and where, who married whom, who had what children, and when and where they lived and died. Ask about written records, such as letters, diaries, photographs, obituaries, holy books with inscriptions, and birth, death, marriage, or baptismal certificates. In short, begin by gathering as much information as you can from your own family.

Then sketch out your family tree (or pedigree chart). You can do it by hand or on genealogy software from the Internet. An excellent Web site to help you get started is at *www.familyhistory. org*. It has loads of free software, step-by-step instructions for beginners, and more ideas about researching your family history than can possibly be included here, including links to many Mexican sources.

Keep your list of questions handy and revise them as your research goes forward. The Internet has so much information that it can be easy to get lost. Don't get so buried in information that you forget the original questions, and don't be so stuck on your original questions that you neglect to ask new ones! Keep your records and research notes organized, thorough, and up to date, and remember: Only by asking good, specific questions will researchers get the answers they are looking for.

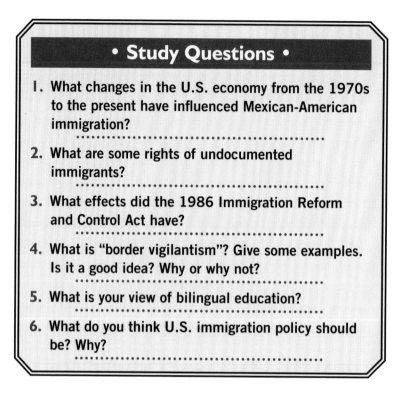

• Study Questions •

1. What changes in the U.S. economy from the 1970s to the present have influenced Mexican-American immigration?
....

2. What are some rights of undocumented immigrants?
....

3. What effects did the 1986 Immigration Reform and Control Act have?
....

4. What is "border vigilantism"? Give some examples. Is it a good idea? Why or why not?
....

5. What is your view of bilingual education?
....

6. What do you think U.S. immigration policy should be? Why?
....

9

Changing America

The debate about illegal Mexican-American immigration continues to rage, and the two sides are extremely different in their views.

One side is represented by a scholar named Samuel Huntington. In his book *Who Are We? The Challenges to America's National Identity* (2004), Huntington argued that Mexican immigration poses huge dangers to the country. More specifically, he argued that:

- Mexican Americans and other Latinos are not assimilating as did past generations of European immigrants. Instead, they tend to keep their languages, cultures, and allegiances to families and communities in their home countries.

- There are several reasons for this. The number of recently arrived Latinos is much larger than any group of

Europeans. Their home countries are much nearer, and their culture is much different. Many feel no attachment to America's "Anglo-Protestant culture" or even hostility toward it.

• Massive Mexican and Latino immigration threatens America's core values and beliefs. It is creating two nations in the United States: those who identify as Americans and embrace America's core values and those who do not.

Huntington represents one side in this debate. Another side is represented by scholars like Richard Alba and Victor Nee. In their book *Remaking the American Mainstream* (2003), Alba and Nee argued that Latino immigrants are behaving similarly to past generations of European immigrants. More specifically, they argued that:

• Assimilation has always been a two-way street. Just as past waves of immigrants have adopted many features of their new country, so the dominant culture has changed in response to new arrivals. The same thing is happening today.

• Intermarriage rates, educational and income levels, language use, and other data show that Latino immigrants are assimilating, although not exactly as Europeans did.

• America's core values of political equality and equal opportunity are not in danger, but the idea of "whiteness" probably is. Rising numbers of nonwhite immigrants are changing America's racial makeup. Racial boundaries among whites, blacks, Latinos, and Asians are being replaced by a more inclusive idea of what it means to be an American.

These are two sides of an ongoing debate. Which is right? To decide, look more closely at the evidence in three important areas: (1) language, (2) education and earnings, and (3) intermarriage rates. These are important because many scholars consider them benchmarks of assimilation—that is, they help people decide whether assimilation is occurring.

LANGUAGE

Imagine the United States without a dominant language. How would people communicate? Huntington and others fear that, because Mexican immigrants tend to retain their native tongue, English is in danger of losing its place as the dominant language, the "linguistic glue" that binds the country together. Are their fears justified?

Alba and Nee showed that patterns of English usage by Mexican Americans are similar to those of past generations of European immigrants, with some differences. The typical pattern for Europeans was for first-generation immigrants to speak their native tongue and learn just enough English to get by. Their children learned English at school and continued to speak their parents' language at home, making them bilingual. The third generation (grandchildren of the first) typically spoke only English and lost the bilingualism.

For Mexican immigrants, the patterns are similar, although with more bilingualism. Analysis of the 2000 U.S census shows that 79 percent of first-generation Mexican children spoke English well. In the second generation, 92 percent spoke English well and 85 percent spoke some Spanish at home (they were bilingual). In the third generation, all spoke English well, and 72 percent spoke only English at home—slightly lower than for European immigrants. The most important difference between Mexican Americans and Euro-Americans is that third, fourth, and later generations of Mexican Americans tend to stay bilingual, especially in the borderlands. Alba and Nee did not see this bilingualism as a danger to English continuing as America's linguistic glue.[60]

EDUCATION AND EARNINGS

People on Huntington's side of the debate fear that Latino immigrants will stay poor and unskilled. They foresee the danger of a permanent underclass of poor, uneducated, non-English speakers with little or no allegiance to American ideals.

What does the evidence say? Again, the 2000 U.S. census and other data show a pattern similar to past generations of European immigrants. Overall, each generation of Mexican Americans improves its educational and earnings levels. On average, second-generation Mexican Americans had nearly four years more schooling than their parents and earned about one-third more. For the third generation, schooling increased by about one year and earnings rose slightly. In recent years, the rise in earnings has stalled by the third generation, even as educational levels rise. Alba and Nee attributed this stalling mainly to economic changes since the 1970s and the growing difficulty of finding good, high-paying jobs (see Chapter 8).

Overall, argued Alba and Nee, the evidence does not support the view that the United States is in danger of becoming home to a permanent underclass of poor, unskilled, uneducated third- and fourth-generation Latinos. The desire for more education and higher earnings is shared by just about everyone. The newest arrivals simply need more time and opportunities to achieve their goals, just as past generations of Europeans did.[61] Huntington, in contrast, argued that more time will only widen the gap further.

INTERMARRIAGE

Another key measure of assimilation is intermarriage: How many immigrants and their offspring marry outside their culture?

Huntington and others believe that Mexican Americans tend to marry within their own group, weakening the ties between them and the larger society.

What does the data say? Overall, rates of intermarriage for Mexican Americans are fairly high, but lower than for past generations of European immigrants. Census data show that nearly 30 percent of Mexican-American men and women were married to non–Mexican Americans—about half the rate for Euro-Americans in the mid-twentieth century. The overall trends are similar, however: With each passing generation, intermarriage increases.

Overall, Alba and Nee argue that these and other data show that Mexican Americans are becoming part of the American mainstream. They maintain that, in all three areas, Mexican Americans are assimilating into American society, although not exactly as Europeans did. In any case, the debate continues.

ENDINGS AND BEGINNINGS

You have traveled a long way in this book, from Rita and César Chávez to the dawn of Mexican civilization to some of the many contributions Mexican Americans have made to the culture and society shared by all Americans. The book concludes with some suggestions for how you might continue this journey of discovery on your own.

- **Books.** One of the best ways to learn about anything. Check the Further Reading section and the endnotes and search online. (If your local public library does not have a book you are interested in, they can get it through interlibrary loan. Just ask the library staff how to request a book through interlibrary loan and follow their instructions. This is often also true of educational videos.)

(continues on page 123)

ACCOMPLISHMENTS REACH ACROSS CULTURAL BORDERS

Another element that people on the Huntington side of the debate tend to ignore is the tremendous contributions Mexican Americans have made and are making to American society and culture. Name a job, an occupation, or a field, and it is guaranteed that Mexican Americans have made important contributions to it: science, technology, medicine, culture, every field of human endeavor. Let us look more closely at culture.

Consider music. Radio stations in border states began to play Mexican music as soon as commercial radio was invented in the 1920s—from soulful folk songs and ballads (*corridos* and *rancheros*) to the upbeat rhythms of mariachi and pop. Recent superstars like Tatiana, Ricky Muñoz, and Selena built on a long tradition of musicians like Pedro González and Las Madrugadores ("The Night Owls"); Lydia Mendoza, nicknamed "The Lark of the Border"; Linda Ronstadt; Carlos Santana; and many others. The Latin Grammys, launched in 1999, show that the music industry understands the growing importance of Latin music. Also in recent years, "ballet folklórico" troupes have revived traditional Mexican folk dances, which have become increasingly popular—and not only among Mexican Americans.

Now, consider film. There are so many famous Mexican-American actors, from Dolores del Río of the golden age of silent movies to two-time Academy Award winner Anthony Quinn, who appeared in more than 150 movies over six decades. The steely eyed police captain in the 1980s hit TV series *Miami Vice* was played by Edward James Olmos, who also starred in *The Ballad of Gregorio Cortez* (1982; see Chapter 2) and many other films. Today's Mexican-American stars include Salma Hayek (*Frida*, 2002, and *Spy Kids 3-D: Game Over*, 2003) and Jessica Alba (*Fantastic Four*, 2005).

Mexican-American actress Jessica Alba is pictured here at the 78th Annual Academy Awards in March 2006. Alba has starred in a number of movies, including *Sin City* (2005) and *Fantastic Four* (2005).

The film *La Bamba* (1987) traced the short life of Mexican-American pop music sensation Ritchie Valens, who died in a plane crash at age 17 and whose hit song "La Bamba" (1957) fused Mexican-American rhythms to American pop. Valens was inducted into the Rock and Roll Hall of Fame in 2001. Many other movies, like the hysterically funny *The Milagro Beanfield War* (1988; though the book is even funnier!) and *Stand and Deliver* (1988) explore diverse aspects of the Mexican-American experience. Prominent Chicano film directors include Gregory Nava (*El Norte*, 1983, *Selena*, 1997) and Luis Valdez (*Zoot Suit*, 1981, *La Bamba*, 1987). These and dozens of others have made enduring contributions to American cinema.

Painters and muralists have also contributed to this flowering of visual art. Los Angeles alone is home to more than 1,000 public murals, including the longest mural in the world, the Great Wall of Los Angeles, which stretches more than half a mile. Painted in bold, vibrant colors, many with social and cultural themes, these murals tell stories about Mexican-American history and

(continues on next page)

(continued from previous page)

identity, beliefs and struggles, hopes and dreams. Artists like Judy Baca—the head of the Great Wall project—Manuel Martínez, and hundreds of others have given visual form to the Mexican-American experience. Many photographers, sculptors, and performance artists, like the totally wacky Guillermo Gómez-Peña, also have made valuable contributions to American culture.

What about literature? Here the field is exceptionally rich, with scores of highly accomplished writers, poets, and play-wrights. You have been introduced to some, like Sandra Cisne-ros, Richard Rodriguez, and Patricia Preciado Martin. To these could be added Rudolfo Anaya, whose haunting novel *Bless Me, Ultima* (1972) stands among the best of American fiction; Gary Soto, whose stories for children and young adults con-tinue to enrapture thousands; and Mary Helen Ponce, whose stories and novels capture life's magic and mysteries. Young readers would easily find enough excellent fiction by Mexican-American authors to keep them happily occupied for a very long time.

Scholarship? Mexican-American scholars have made last-ing contributions to every field of human knowledge, from chemistry and physics to history and anthropology. Sports? Name a sport, and Mexican Americans likely rank among the top players.

Finally, think about the Mexican holidays that many celebrate as American holidays. Who has not heard of Cinco de Mayo? (This holiday commemorates the victory of the Mexican Army over the French invaders on May 5, 1862.) More and more, people with no Mexican ancestry are participating in Mexico-oriented holidays and cultural events, like Las Posadas, concerts, plays, dance, mu-seums, art exhibits, and more.

Even this very brief survey should reveal that Mexican Ameri-cans have made and are making tremendous contributions to the best of American culture.

(continued from page 119)

- **Movies.** On top of those already mentioned, see *Salt of the Earth* (1954, one of the finest films ever made); *El Mariachi* (1992), *Like Water for Chocolate* (1993), *Selena* (1997), *Bread and Roses* (2000), and *Real Women Have Curves* (2002). Some Web site lists are in the Further Reading section.

- **Educational videos.** Some good starting points are in Further Reading.

- **Music.** Many public libraries are musical treasure troves; the possibilities are endless.

- **Museums, concerts, plays, art exhibits.** Check your local newspaper or town/city Web site for cultural events in your area. You can also take virtual tours on the Internet

Many Mexican Americans celebrate Cinco de Mayo, a holiday that marks the Mexican Army's defeat of French troops at the Battle of Puebla on May 5, 1862. Pictured here is Danza Teocalt, a Los Angeles dance group performing during a Cinco de Mayo celebration.

(Google "Mexican American" or "Chicano" and "art," "mural," "theater," etc.).

- **Shops and stores.** Chances are good that there is a Mexican-American grocery store near you. Go see what they sell. Take note of unfamiliar foods. Talk to the workers and owners or get a Mexican cookbook and try some new recipes—cooking new dishes can be as fun as eating them.

- **Friends and neighbors.** If you are not Mexican American yourself, it is likely that some of your neighbors, classmates, or friends are. With their permission, and always respecting people's privacy, ask them about their place of origin, family, religion, food, music, culture—and see where the conversation leads.

- **Learn Spanish.** Learning new languages is much easier for young people than for adults. Did you know that many people around the world grow up speaking three, four, or even five languages? There are kids who speak more languages than their years of age. The human brain, especially the young human brain, is truly an amazing thing. If you are not fluent already, take advantage of your young brain by learning some Spanish. Will it ever come in handy? *Por supuesto!* (Of course!)

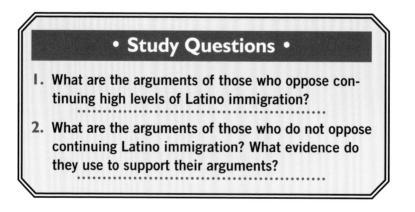

• Study Questions •

1. What are the arguments of those who oppose continuing high levels of Latino immigration?

2. What are the arguments of those who do not oppose continuing Latino immigration? What evidence do they use to support their arguments?

3. Where do you stand on this issue? What do you think the solution is?

....

4. Identify some ways Mexican Americans have contributed to American culture.

....

5. What is *your* plan of action for learning more about the Mexican-American experience?

....

Chronology

5000 B.C.	Natives in central and southern Mexico domesticate maize (corn).
1000 B.C.– A.D. 1521	A series of civilizations rise and fall in what are now central and southern Mexico and the U.S. Southwest.
A.D. 1325	The Aztecs (or Mexica) migrate from northern Mexico, settle on a small island in Lake Texcoco in the Valley of Mexico.

Timeline

1821
Mexico gains its independence from Spain

1910–1920
More than 250,000 Mexicans migrate to the United States during Mexican Revolution

1942–1965
Bracero Program sends workers from Mexico to the United States

1821

1942

1846–1848
Mexican-American War fought between the United States and Mexico

1930–1939
Many Mexicans and Mexican Americans forced to return to Mexico due to the weak U.S. economy

1426	The Aztecs become the dominant power in the Valley of Mexico.
1520	At least 25 million natives populate central and southern Mexico.
1521	The Spanish conquer the Aztecs and destroy their capital city and empire; natives become Indians.
1531	Mexican Indian Juan Diego sees a vision of a dark-skinned virgin who later becomes the Virgin of Guadalupe.
1607	The first permanent English settlement in North America is founded at Jamestown.
1608	Santa Fe is founded in New Mexico.
1650	Mexico's Indian population plummets to less than one million.

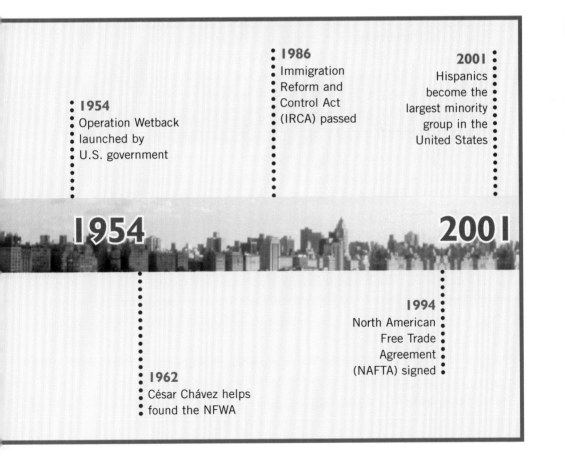

1986
Immigration
Reform and
Control Act
(IRCA) passed

2001
Hispanics
become the
largest minority
group in the
United States

1954
Operation Wetback
launched by
U.S. government

1954

2001

1994
North American
Free Trade
Agreement
(NAFTA) signed

1962
César Chávez helps
found the NFWA

1783   The United States is recognized as an independent country.

1810   On the night of September 15, Father Miguel Hidalgo begins the struggle for Mexican independence; the next day, September 16, is now celebrated as Mexican Independence Day, even though real independence did not come for 11 years.

1821   Mexico becomes an independent country.

1836   Texas declares independence from Mexico.

1836–1845   Texas is an independent country.

1846–1848   The Mexican-American War, between the United States and Mexico, is waged.

1848   The Treaty of Guadalupe Hidalgo ends the Mexican-American War and grants the United States the northern two-fifths of Mexico.

1862   On May 5, the Mexican Army defeats the French invaders; this date is later celebrated as the national holiday Cinco de Mayo.

1910–1920   The Mexican Revolution; more than 250,000 Mexicans migrate to the United States.

1914–1918   World War I (the United States enters the war in April 1917).

1930–1939   The Great Depression affects the economy; forced repatriation campaigns send many Mexican Americans back to Mexico.

1939–1945   World War II (the United States enters the war in December 1941).

1942–1965   The Bracero Program sends workers from Mexico to the United States.

1954   The U.S. government launches Operation Wetback.

1962   The National Farm Workers of America (NFWA), first meets in Fresno, California.

1965–1970   The NFWA strikes against California grape growers.

1965–1975 The Chicano years.

1969 The first Chicano Youth Conference meets in Denver.

1986 The Immigration Reform and Control Act (IRCA) is passed.

1994 The North American Free Trade Agreement (NAFTA), between Canada, the United States, and Mexico, is signed; California voters approve Proposition 187.

2001 Hispanics—more than two-thirds of whom are Mexican Americans—become the largest minority group in the United States.

Notes

Chapter 1

1. Jacques E. Levy, *Cesar Chavez* (New York: W. W. Norton & Company, 1975), 20.
2. Available online at *www.sfsu.edu/~cecipp/cesar_chavez/cesar's_death.htm*
3. Ibid., 18.
4. Available online at *www.chavezfoundation.org.*
5. Ibid., 20.

Chapter 2

6. A classic study of Mexican-American migration to the United States is Carey McWilliams, *North From Mexico* (New York: Greenwood Press, 1948). A very good collection of original documents from before World War I is David J. Weber, ed., *Foreigners in Their Native Land* (Albuquerque: University of New Mexico Press, 1973). Mexican Americans who tell their migration stories are collected in Manuel Gamio, *The Life Story of the Mexican Immigrant* (New York: Dover Publications, 1971). The story of folk hero Gregorio Cortez is told in Américo Paredes', *With a Pistol in His Hand* (Austin: University of Texas Press, 1971).

Chapter 3

7. The standard college textbook on Mexican history is Michael C. Meyer, William L. Sherman, and Susan M. Deeds, *The Course of Mexican History* (New York: Oxford University Press, 2002). Your local public library probably has many good books on Mexico, many written for middle schoolers. Two examples are Elizabeth Coonrod Martinez, *Coming to America: The Mexican-American Experience* (Brookfield, Conn.: Millbrook Press, 1995), and Frank De Varona, *Miguel Hidaldo y Costilla: Father of Mexican Independence* (Brookfield, Conn.: Millbrook Press, 1993). On the conquest of Mexico, an excellent place to start is the eyewitness account of Bernal Díaz, *The Conquest of Mexico*, trans. J. M. Cohen (Baltimore: Penguin Books, 1963). On Mexican poverty and migration rates see "Mexico Growth Failing to Combat Poverty—OECD," Reuters, September 12, 2005.

Chapter 4

8. Rubén Martínez, *Crossing Over* (New York: Metropolitan Books, 2001), 34.
9. Ibid., 31.

10. "The Business of the Future: Banks, Latinos, and the Changing Financial Borders," Available online at *http://utopia.utexas. edu/articles/tbr/banks_latinos. html?sec=business&sub=finance.*

11. Information in this section from Martínez, *Crossing Over*, and Mike Davis, *Magical Urbanism* (London: Verso, 2001), chapter 4.

12. *New York Times*, October 16, 2002.

13. Jorge Ramos, *Dying to Cross* (New York: HarperCollins, 2005).

14. Denis Lynn Daly Heyck, *Barrios and Borderlands* (London: Routledge, 1994).

15. Ibid., 205.

16. Ibid., 206.

17. Ibid., 206.

18. Ibid., 208.

19. Ibid., 212.

20. Martínez, *Crossing Over*, xx.

21. Sandra Cisneros, *The House on Mango Street* (New York: Vintage, 1984), 4.

22. Ibid., 9.

23. Ibid., 10.

24. Ibid., 28.

25. Ibid., 33.

26. Laurie Kay Sommers in collaboration with Casa de Unidad Cultural Arts and Media Center, *Fiesta, Fe, y Cultura: Celebrations of Faith and Culture in Detroit's Colonia Mexicana* (Detroit: Casa de Unidad Cultural Arts and Media Center, and East Lansing: Michigan State University Museum, 1995), 4

27. Ibid., 15.

Chapter 5

28. The term *MexAmerica* is taken from Lester D. Langley's book, *MexAmerica* (New York: Crown, 1988).

29. On Mexican Canadians, see "Canada: Ag Guest Workers," *http://migration.ucdavis. edu/rmn/more.php?id=547_ 0_4_0*; and *www.workpermit. com/news/2005_05_04/canada/*. See also the documentary film *El Contrato: The Contract* (2003), which follows the lives of Mexican tomato workers in Leamington, Ontario.

30. The information in the following section is adapted from: United States Census Bureau, "The Hispanic Population: Census 2000 Brief," May 2001; United States Census Bureau, "The Hispanic Population in the United States: March 2002"; Jeffrey Passel, "Mexican Immigration to the US: The Latest Estimates," Migration Information Source, March 1, 2004; Elizabeth Grieco, "The Foreign Born from Mexico in the United States," Migration Information Source, October 1, 2003.

Chapter 6

31. Quoted in Carlos Muñoz, Jr., *Youth, Identity, Power* (London: Verso, 1989), 22–23.

32. Quote from Dick Meister, "The Farmworkers' Angry Champion," November 5, 2004, Available online at *www.eopinions. com/content_4141326468*.

33. Quote from Arthur F. Corwin, "Mexican-American History: An Assessment," in *The Chicano*, edited by Norris Hundley, Jr. (Santa Barbara, Calif.: Clio Press, 1975), 23.

34. John Womack, "A Special Supplement: The Chicanos," the *New York Review of Books*, August 31, 1972, Available online at *www.nybooks.com/articles/10103*.

35. Ernesto Galarza, *Barrio Boy* (Notre Dame, Ind.: University of Notre Dame Press, 1971), 2.

36. Richard Rodriguez, *Hunger of Memory* (New York: Bantam Books, 1982), 115.

37. On LULAC's founding and history, see the organization's Web site at *www.lulac.org*; on LULAC's successes and limitations, see Rodolfo Acuña, *Occupied America*, 2nd edition. (New York: Harper & Row, 1981), 309–310.

38. Cynthia E. Orozco, "Alice Dickerson Montemayor: Feminism and Mexican American Politics in the 1930s," in *Writing the Range: Race, Class, and Culture in the Women's West*, edited by Elizabeth Jameson and Susan Armitage (Norman: University of Oklahoma Press, 1997), 443.

Chapter 7

39. On Tijerina and the Alianza, see Patricia Bell Blawis, *Tijerina and the Land Grants* (New York: International Publishers, 1971); "Reies López Tijerina"

in *Readings on La Raza*, edited by Matt S. Meier and Feliciano Ribera (New York: Hill and Wang, 1974), 236–243, and their book, *Mexican Americans/ American Mexicans* (New York: Hill and Wang, 1993), 212–214.

40. On La Raza Unida see Muñoz, *Youth, Identity, Power*, chapter 4; Armando Navarro, *The Cristal Experiment* (Madison: University of Wisconsin Press, 1998); "La Raza Unida," in The Handbook of Texas Online, *www.tsha.utexas.edu/handbook/ online/articles/*.

41. Corinn Codye, *Vilma Martínez* (Austin, Tex.: Steck Vaughn Co., 1993); biographies at *www. latinohistory.com* and *www. abanet.org*.

Chapter 8

42. Martis, "#187 Illegal Aliens," 1; "Payments to Help Hospitals Care for Illegal Immigrants," *New York Times*, May 10, 2005.

43. "Time to Fix Immigration," (editorial), *New York Times*, October 14, 2005.

44. Pia M. Orrenius and Madeline Zavodny, "Do Amnesty Programs Encourage Illegal Immigration? Evidence from the Immigration Reform and Control Act (IRCA)," Federal Reserve Bank of Atlanta, Working Paper 2001-19, November 2001, 15.

45. "California Proposition 187," *http://wikisource.org/*

46. Nancy H. Martis, "#187 Illegal Aliens. Ineligibility for public

services. Verification and Reporting "*California Journal,* 1994, *www.calvoter.org/archive/ 94general/props/187.html.* See also Davis, *Magical Urbanism,* chapter 9.

47. Timothy Egan, "A Battle Against Illegal Workers With an Un- likely Driving Force," *New York Times,* May 30, 2005.

48. Ibid.

49. Timothy Egan, "Wanted: Border Hoppers. And Some Excite- ment, Too," *New York Times,* April 1, 2005.

50. Susy Buchanan and David Holthouse, "Playing Rough," *Intelligence Report,* Southern Poverty Law Center, Fall 2005, 42–49.

51. "Border Patrol Considering Use of Volunteers, Official Says," *New York Times,* July 21, 2005.

52. Simon Romero, "Patrolling the Border for Migrants From Mexico, With a Humanitarian Goal," *New York Times,* July 20, 2005.

53. Paul Vitello, "As Illegal Work- ers Hit Suburbs, Politicians Scramble to Respond," *New York Times,* October 6, 2005.

54. Pam Belluck, "Town Uses Trespass Law to Fight Illegal Immigrants," *New York Times,* July 13, 2005.

55. "Up to 64 Laborers Lived in a Small House, Authorities Say," *New York Times,* June 21, 2005.

56. Shaila Dewan, "Immigrants in Tennessee Get Certificates to Drive," *New York Times,* May 9, 2005.

57. William Yardley, "New Haven Mayor Ponders ID Cards for Illegal Migrants," *New York Times,* October 8, 2005.

58. "Housing Discrimination 'Alive and Well' in Alameda," *People's Weekly World,* October 30, 2004, *www.pww.org/article/articlev- iew/6022/1/238.*

59. Gary Orfield and Chungmei Lee, "New Faces, Old Patterns? Segregation in the Multiracial South," Civil Rights Project, Harvard University, *www. civilrightsproject.harvard.edu.* See also "Latinos Segregated 50 Years After Brown v. Board of Education," Associated Press, April 6, 2004.

Chapter 9

60. Richard Alba, "Bilingual- ism Persists, But English Still Predominates," Migration Information Source, February 1, 2005, *www.migrationin- formation.org/Feature/print. cfm?ID=282.*

61. Walter A. Ewing, "Immigrant Success or Stagnation? Con- fronting the Claim of Latino Non-Advancement," American Immigration Law Foundation, 2003, *www.ailf.org/ipc/Succes- sOrStagnation.html.*

Glossary

Alianza (ah-lee-ON-za)   The Alianza Federal de Pueblos Libres (Federal Alliance of Land Grants) founded by Reies López Tijerina in New Mexico in 1963.

Anglo   An English-speaking person of European ancestry in the United States.

Aztecs   The native civilization and empire based in the Valley of Mexico before the Spanish conquest.

Aztlán (oz-TLON)   The mythical homeland of Chicanos, somewhere in the American Southwest.

barrio (BAH-ree-oh)   A Mexican-American neighborhood.

bilingual education   Teaching schoolchildren in both their native language and their adopted language.

borderlands   A large section of northern Mexico and the American Southwest that straddles the border and has a distinctive history and culture because of the border.

bracero (bra-SAY-ro)   A Mexican worker temporarily in the United States between 1942 and 1965; from the Spanish *brazo* ("arm"), roughly translates as "helping hand."

californios (col-ee-FORN-yos)   Descendants of Spanish settlers in California.

Chicana   A female Chicano.

Chicano (chee-KAHN-oh)   Derived from "Mexicano." A person of Mexican ancestry (also spelled *Xicano*).

coyote (coy-OH-tay)   A paid smuggler of undocumented migrants across the U.S. border.

Crusade for Justice   The Mexican-American civil rights organization founded by Corky Gonzales in Denver in 1965.

greaser   A racist Anglo term of abuse and insult toward Mexican Americans.

hacienda (ah-see-END-ah) A large, privately owned Mexican farm.

Hispanic A person who can trace his or her ancestry to Iberia (Spain and Portugal); U.S. Census Bureau definition in 2000: a person of any race of Latin-American ancestry.

hispanos (ee-SPAHN-os) Descendants of Spanish settlers in New Mexico and Colorado.

illegal alien An undocumented migrant.

la migra (la MEE-grah) The Spanish nickname for the U.S. Border Patrol and (former) Immigration and Naturalization Service (INS).

la raza The people.

La Raza Unida (la RAH-za oo-NEE-dah) "The People United," a Chicano political party founded in 1970 in Crystal City, Texas.

Latino A person who can trace his or her ancestry to Latin America.

LULAC The League of United Latin American Citizens.

machismo (ma-CHEEZ-mo) The shared idea among Mexican men about how they should act: "with manliness"; a gender role in which men dominate women.

maize Corn; in Spanish, *maíz* **(mah-EEZ)**.

MALDEF The Mexican American Legal Defense and Educational Fund.

marianismo (mah-ree-on-EEZ-mo) The shared idea among Mexicans about how women should behave and obey men.

mestizo (meh-STEE-zo) A person of mixed Indian and Spanish ancestry.

National Farm Workers Association (NFWA) The union formed by César Chávez and the farmworkers in California in the early 1960s.

other side, the The United States.

PRI (pree) *Partido Revolucionario Institutional* (Institutional Revolutionary Party); the ruling party in Mexico from 1929 to 2000.

remittances Money earned and sent by migrants working in another country to their families and communities in their home countries.

repatriation   Forcing someone to return to his or her country of origin.

tejano (tay-HAH-no)   A Texan of Mexican ancestry.

undocumented migrant   Someone who has moved to another country without a visa, passport, or other legal requirements (same as "unauthorized migrant" and similar to "illegal alien").

vaquero (va-KAY-ro)   A Mexican cowboy.

wetback   A term of abuse and insult against Mexican Americans.

Xicano   Same as "Chicano."

Bibliography

Acuña, Rodolfo. *Occupied America*, 2nd edition. New York: Harper & Row, 1981.

Alba, Richard. "Bilingualism Persists, But English Still Predominates." Migration Information Source, February 1, 2005. Available online at *www.migrationinformation.org*.

———, and Victor Nee. *Remaking the American Mainstream: Assimilation and Contemporary Immigration*. Cambridge, Mass.: Harvard University Press, 2003.

Associated Press. "Latinos Segregated 50 Years After Brown v. Board of Education." April 6, 2004.

Blawis, Patricia Bell. *Tijerina and the Land Grants*. New York: International Publishers, 1971.

Border Action Network. "Hate or Heroism: Vigilantes on the Arizona-Mexico Border." December 2002. Available online at *www.borderaction.org*.

"Border Patrol Considering Use of Volunteers, Official Says." *New York Times*, July 21, 2005.

Buchanan, Susy, and David Holthouse. "Playing Rough." *Intelligence Report*, Southern Poverty Law Center, Fall 2005, pp. 42–49.

"Business of the Future: Banks, Latinos, and the Changing Financial Borders." Available online at *http://utopia.utexas.edu*.

"Canada: Ag Guest Workers." Available online at *http://migration.ucdavis.edu* and *www.workpermit.com*.

Cisneros, Sandra. *The House on Mango Street*. New York: Vintage, 1984.

Codye, Corinn. *Vilma Martínez*. Austin, Tex.: Steck Vaughn Co., 1993.

Davis, Mike. *Magical Urbanism*. London: Verso, 2001.

Dewan, Shaila. "Immigrants in Tennessee Get Certificates to Drive." *New York Times*, May 9, 2005.

Díaz, Bernal. *The Conquest of Mexico*, trans. J. M. Cohen. Baltimore: Penguin Books, 1963.

Egan, Timothy. "Wanted: Border Hoppers. And Some Excitement, Too." *New York Times*, April 1, 2005.

———. "A Battle Against Illegal Workers in Idaho Has an Unlikely Driving Force." *New York Times*, May 30, 2005.

Ellingwood, Ken. *Hard Line.* New York: Pantheon, 2004.

Ewing, Walter A. "Immigrant Success or Stagnation? Confronting the Claim of Latino Non-Advancement." American Immigration Law Foundation, 2003. Available online at *www.ailf.org/ipc/SuccessOrStagnation.html.*

Ferriss, Susan, and Ricardo Sandoval. *The Fight in the Fields.* New York: Harcourt Brace, 1997.

Galarza, Ernesto. *Barrio Boy.* Notre Dame, Ind.: University of Notre Dame Press, 1971.

Gamio, Manuel. *The Life Story of the Mexican Immigrant.* New York: Dover Publications, 1971.

Grieco, Elizabeth. "The Foreign Born from Mexico in the United States." Migration Information Source, October 1, 2003.

Heyck, Denis Lynn Daly. *Barrios and Borderlands.* London: Routledge, 1994.

Hundley, Jr., Norris, ed. *The Chicano.* Santa Barbara, Calif.: Clio Press, 1975.

Huntington, Samuel P. *Who Are We? The Challenges to American Identity.* New York: Simon & Schuster, 2004.

Langley, Lester D. *MexAmerica.* New York: Crown, 1988.

"La Raza Unida." *The Handbook of Texas Online.* Available online at *www.tsha.utexas.edu/handbook/online/articles/.*

Levy, Jacques E. *Cesar Chavez.* New York: W. W. Norton & Company, 1975.

Martínez, Rubén. *Crossing Over: A Mexican Family on the Migrant Trail.* New York: Metropolitan Books, 2001.

Martis, Nancy H. "#187 Illegal Aliens. Ineligibility for Public Services. Verification and Reporting." *California Journal,* 1994. Available online at *www.calvoter.org/archive/94general/props/187.html.*

McWilliams, Carey. *North From Mexico.* New York: Greenwood Press, 1948.

Meier, Matt S., and Feliciano Ribera, eds. *Readings on La Raza.* New York: Hill & Wang, 1974.

———. eds. *Mexican Americans/American Mexicans.* New York: Hill & Wang, 1993.

Meister, Dick. "The Farmworker's Angry Champion." November 5, 2004. Available online at *www.eopinions.com/content_4141326468.*

Meyer, Michael C., William L. Sherman, and Susan M. Deeds. *The Course of Mexican History.* New York: Oxford University Press, 2002.

Muñoz, Carlos, Jr. *Youth, Identity, Power.* London: Verso, 1989.

Navarro, Armando. *The Cristal Experiment.* Madison: University of Wisconsin Press, 1998.

Orfield, Gary, and Chungmei Lee. "New Faces, Old Patterns? Segregation in the Multiracial South." Civil Rights Project, Harvard University. Available online at *www.civilrightsproject.harvard.edu.*

Orozco, Cynthia E. "Alice Dickerson Montemayor: Feminism and Mexican American Politics in the 1930s," in *Writing the Range: Race, Class, and Culture in the Women's West,* edited by Elizabeth Jameson and Susan Armitage. Norman: University of Oklahoma Press, 1997, pp. 435–466.

Orrenius, Pia M., and Madeline Zavodny. "Do Amnesty Programs Encourage Illegal Immigration? Evidence from the Immigration Reform and Control Act (IRCA)." Federal Reserve Bank of Atlanta, Working Paper 2001-19, Nov. 2001.

Paredes, Américo. *With a Pistol in His Hand.* Austin: University of Texas Press, 1971.

Passel, Jeffrey. "Mexican Immigration to the US: The Latest Estimates." Migration Information Source, March 1, 2004.

Pear, Robert. "Payments to Help Hospitals Care for Illegal Immigrants." *New York Times,* May 10, 2005.

People's Weekly World. "Housing Discrimination 'Alive and Well' in Alameda." October 30, 2004. Available online at *www.pww.org/article/articleview/ 6022/1/238.*

Ramos, Jorge. *Dying to Cross.* New York: HarperCollins, 2005.

Rodriguez, Richard. *Hunger of Memory.* New York: Bantam Books, 1982.

Romero, Simon. "Patrolling the Border for Migrants From Mexico, With a Humanitarian Goal." *New York Times,* July 20, 2005.

Ross, Fred. *Conquering Goliath*. Keene, Calif.: United Farm Workers, 1989.

Sommers, Laurie Kay, in collaboration with Casa de Unidad Cultural Arts and Media Center. *Fiesta, Fe, y Cultura: Celebrations of Faith and Culture in Detroit's Colonia Mexicana*. Detroit: Casa de Unidad Cultural Arts and Media Center, and East Lansing: Michigan State University Museum, 1995.

Southern Poverty Law Center. "Center Team Crushes Border Vigilantes." *SPLC Report*, September 2005.

"Time to Fix Immigration" (editorial). *New York Times*, October 14, 2005.

"Town Uses Trespass Law to Fight Illegal Immigrants." *New York Times*, July 13, 2005.

Tracy, Kathleen. *Cesar Chavez*. Bear, Del.: Mitchell Lane Publishers, 2004.

United States Census Bureau. "The Hispanic Population: Census 2000 Brief," May 2001.

United States Census Bureau. "The Hispanic Population in the United States: March 2002."

"Up to 64 Laborers Lived in a Small House, Authorities Say." *New York Times*, June 21, 2005.

Urrea, Luis Alberto. *The Devil's Highway*. New York: Little, Brown, 2004.

Vitello, Paul. "As Illegal Workers Hit Suburbs, Politicians Scramble to Respond." *New York Times*, October 6, 2005.

Weber, David J., ed. *Foreigners in Their Native Land*. Albuquerque: University of New Mexico Press, 1973.

Womack, John. "A Special Supplement: The Chicanos." *The New York Review of Books*, August 31, 1972. Available online at *www.nybooks.com/articles/10103*.

Yardley, William. "New Haven Mayor Ponders ID Cards for Illegal Migrants." *New York Times*, October 8, 2005.

Further Reading

Canales, Viola. *Orange Candy and Other Secret Tales.* Houston, Tex.: Piñata Books, 2001.

Castillo Guilbault, Rose. *Farmworker's Daughter: Growing Up Mexican in America.* Berkeley, Calif.: Heyday Books, 2005.

Jiménez, Francisco. *The Circuit: Stories from the Life of a Migrant Child.* Boston: Houghton Mifflin Co., 1999.

Martínez, Manuel Luis. *Drift.* New York: Picador, 2003.

Pearce, Kenneth. *A Traveler's History of Mexico.* New York: Interlink Books, 2004.

Rice, David. *Crazy Loco: Stories.* New York: Dial Books, 2001.

Sanchez, Alex. *So Hard To Say.* New York: Simon & Schuster, 2004.

Santana, Patricia. *Motorcycle Ride on the Sea of Tranquility.* Albuquerque: University of New Mexico Press, 2002.

Soto, Gary. *Jessie de la Cruz: A Profile of a United Farm Worker.* New York: Persea Books, 2000.

EDUCATIONAL VIDEOS

Chicano! The History of the Mexican-American Civil Rights Movement, four-part series. NLCC Educational Media, 1996.

Fight in the Fields: Cesar Chavez and the Farmworkers' Struggle. Independent Television Service, 1997.

WEB SITES

César Chávez Foundation
http://www.chavezfoundation.org/

The Julián Samora Research Institute, Michigan State University
www.jsri.msu.edu

Justice for Migrant Workers
www.justice4migrantworkers.org

Iowa State University's Hispanic Heritage Site
www.lib.iastate.edu/commons/hhm/video.html

The Library of Congress
www.loc.gov

League of United Latin American Citizens
http://www.lulac.org/

Mexican American Legal Defense and Educational Fund
www.maldef.org

**National Council of La Raza—Latino Civil Rights and Advocacy
    Organization**
www.nclr.org

Picture Credits

Index

About the Contributors

Series Editor **Robert D. Johnston** is associate professor and director of the Teaching of History Program in the Department of History at the University of Illinois at Chicago. He is the author of *The Making of America: The History of the United States from 1492 to the Present*, a middle-school textbook that received a *School Library Journal* Best Book of the Year award. He is currently working on a history of vaccine controversies in American history, to be published by Oxford University Press.

Michael J. Schroeder received his Ph.D. in history from the University of Michigan in 1993. An award-winning scholar who has published many chapters and articles on Nicaraguan history, he has taught Latino studies and U.S., Mexican, and Latin-American history at the University of Michigan–Flint and Eastern Michigan University. This is his first book.